SELF-GUIDED SHADOW WORK FOR BEGINNERS

A WORKBOOK and JOURNAL
For Profound Self-Discovery
and Powerful Breakthrough Moments

LEIGH W. HART

4 0 1
—Publishing—

Table of Contents

My GIFT to you!

Elevate Your Journey...
with BONUS
Complimentary Support Materials

GIFT #1: Self-Assessment Tests & Bonus Materials

As you begin your shadow work journey, are you unsure where to focus your efforts? Use the self-assessment tests to determine which areas of your life need the most attention.

GIFT #2: Sneak Peek, plus 10 Advanced Shadow Work Exercises

Get a sneak peek inside "Advanced Self-Guided Shadow Work" to continue your journey with an even deeper exploration into your shadow's subconscious. Includes: 10 Advanced Shadow Work exercises!

GIFT #3: The Evolving Growth Workbook

Personal growth is a lifelong journey. Use this workbook now and in the future to revisit insights learned, reevaluate your progress, and continue evolving on your path to personal fulfillment.

Go to:
ShadowWork.LeighWHart.com
to receive your BONUS
printable support materials.

Trigger Warning:

This book explores the depths of the human psyche through the process of shadow work. While this transformative journey can be profoundly healing, it may also bring to the surface challenging and triggering thoughts or emotions. Topics covered in this book may include but are not limited to: trauma, inner conflicts, and unresolved emotions.

We encourage you to engage with this material at your own pace and discretion. If at any point you find yourself feeling overwhelmed or in need of support, please consider reaching out to a mental health professional or a trusted person in your life. Your well-being is of utmost importance.

Remember that you have the power to pause, reflect, and seek assistance whenever you feel it's necessary. You're not alone on this path, and there is help available.

Introduction

Have you ever had someone say to you, "I understand how you feel," and wonder how? There is no way for another person to understand your emotions, your pain, your frustration...your anything because it belongs only to you.

I will not utter those words, but I do empathize, and I want to help you better understand. As you stand on the edge of shadow work, it's natural to feel a sense of apprehension. The term itself can evoke feelings of ominousness and uncertainty, sending a shiver down your spine. It's okay to feel this way. I want you to know that it is normal.

Let's talk about Liz, who, in many ways, reflects the struggles that may have led you here today. Liz found herself trapped in an endless cycle of unhealthy relationships, constantly repeating patterns that left her feeling shattered and adrift. She made choices that led her down a destructive path, sometimes teetering on the edge of addiction. Her yearning for a way out was palpable.

Liz went to a few sessions of therapy, but finances limited her time there. She had grappled with these struggles for years, feeling isolated in her pain. The thought of exploring her shadows was exhausting, and she wondered if it might only bring more darkness into her life.

But then something shifted. Liz decided to take a chance on shadow work, just as you are considering now. As she started down this path, she began to notice small, positive shifts in her life. The overwhelming weight of her past started to lift slowly but surely. She realized that she could move forward at her own pace, creating support systems to navigate this journey of self-discovery on her own.

Now, let's talk about you. You may be facing things similar to Liz, struggling to control a torrent of unwanted emotions—anxiety, fear, guilt, sadness, exhaustion, and perhaps even depression. You've been searching for answers, yearning for personal growth and self-healing, but traditional paths may seem out of reach or overwhelming. The concept of shadow work can be intimidating and laden with questions and uncertainties.

Is shadow work safe? Is it ethical, helpful, and a positive experience? Can you do it on your own? How do you safeguard against re-traumatization? How do you cope with the fear and anxiety that often accompany this process? How can you track your progress, and what do you do if you feel stuck?

I want to assure you that all these questions will be addressed within the pages of this workbook. This is a secure and safe space for you to explore your shadow self and navigate the challenges that arise. Many others have walked this path before you, emerging on the other side with increased strength and self-awareness.

So, what led you to pick up this book? It is quite possible your longing for change, your desire to break free from binding patterns, and your yearning for a brighter, healthier future. If this is why you're here, I want you to know I support you.

By reading and using this workbook, you will acquire practical tools and insights that will help you to:

- ✓ Be guided on how to start shadow work, even as a beginner.

- ✓ Structure your self-analysis for maximum effectiveness.

- ✓ Identify and understand your shadow self.

- ✓ Cultivate self-acceptance and forgiveness.

- ✓ Harness the power of affirmations.

- ✓ Navigate self-guided therapy with confidence.

- ✓ Safely explore and heal past traumas.

In this moment, I want you to envision a life where you are in control of your emotions and where you no longer feel overwhelmed by anxiety, fear, or guilt. Picture yourself making choices that nurture your well-being, freeing yourself from the shackles of your past, and making your own path to a safe, peaceful future.

As the author, I come to you with a background in psychology and personal development, committed to providing you with credible, easy-to-follow guidance. I see you and the difficulties you face in finding your way to the life you deserve, and that's precisely what I aim to provide.

In this workbook, you'll find 80% practical tips and workbook activities that you can immediately put into practice, backed by 10% research and studies supporting the information and complemented by 10% relatable stories that resonate with your experiences.

Together, we will illuminate the shadows, carve the path ahead, and empower you to reclaim control over your life. This is the right book for you, and I'm eager to accompany you on this transformative adventure.

Let's get started.

CHAPTER 1
MASKS AND SHADOWS

Masks and Shadows

> " *The shadow is needed now more than ever. We heal the world when we heal ourselves, and hope shines brightest when it illuminates the dark.* **–Sasha Graham**

We're about to start a trip into the world of shadow work together, exploring the depths of our inner selves step-by-step. This chapter is like the solid ground beneath your feet, providing the foundation you need to begin.

But what exactly is shadow work? Don't worry; I intend to keep this as simple as possible. Shadow work is a process rooted in the ideas of Carl Jung, a famous psychologist. It's all about shining a light on the parts of us we've kept hidden or ignored—those bits that might make us uncomfortable or that we've labeled as bad or unacceptable (Villines, 2022).

Here's the good news: Shadow work isn't about blaming ourselves, feeling broken, or thinking we're strange. It's not about making us feel ashamed or judged. Instead, it's a way to discover more about ourselves, be kind to ourselves, and become better versions of who we already are. It's about acknowledging that we all have shadows, and that's okay.

As we move through this chapter, I want to give you a background to what shadow work is, Jungian principles, the misconceptions behind the method, and why self-guided shadow work can be beneficial. I'll be your guide, and together, we'll look at practical tips and workbook activities that you can easily use in your life.

John's Encounter With His Shadow: A Personal Journey

It was a solemn day for John. He had just laid his father to rest, and the weight of grief hung heavily in the air. After the funeral, John's family and close relatives gathered at his childhood home for a small celebration of life, seeking solace in shared memories and a few drinks. It was meant to be a time of comfort and connection.

But life often has a way of surprising us, doesn't it?

As the evening wore on, a seemingly innocent comment from his cousin Chuck triggered an unexpected reaction from John. In an instant, he found himself grabbing Chuck's shirt and pulling him close, his voice laced with anger and frustration. It was a side of himself he had never witnessed before—a surge of power, raw and untamed. He felt like a character from a movie, the intimidating mob boss.

John's children offered reassurances, citing his grief as the reason for his outburst, but deep down, he couldn't excuse his own behavior. He knew that this wasn't who he wanted to be.

This, my friend, is what we call "The Shadow."

We all have a tendency to present a carefully curated version of ourselves to the world—an image that's pleasant, agreeable, and socially acceptable, much like tidying up our home before guests arrive. Yet, in the corners of our psyche are those unsavory traits we'd rather keep hidden—anger, jealousy, greed. These aspects of ourselves are like classified files, shuffled away into a folder labeled "My Shadow" and promptly forgotten, banished to the depths of our unconscious minds. And so, our comfort zone remains seemingly intact.

But for John, that moment of intense anger was a wake-up call. It forced him to confront a part of himself he had long suppressed—a part he had consigned to the shadows.

John's journey into shadow work had begun, and it would change his life forever.

Now, you might be wondering, "What exactly is this 'shadow work'?" As I mentioned, it's a concept deeply rooted in Jungian psychology, and it's all about embracing and integrating those hidden aspects of ourselves—the good, the bad, and the ugly. It's not about self-blame or labeling ourselves as broken; instead, it's a path to self-awareness and healing.

So, if you're feeling reluctant, afraid, or alone on this path of shadow work, remember that you're not the only one. Together, we'll navigate the uncharted territory of our inner selves, providing you with a safe and inviting space to explore your shadows, understand them, and ultimately, find a healthier balance within yourself. It's a journey worth taking, and we're here to guide you every step of the way.

The Shadow Self

It is important to distinguish your inner shadow traits, and I have included an exercise on how to embrace your shadow self.

Shadow work exercises are like treasure hunts for the parts of ourselves we've hidden away. The theory behind them is pretty simple: by bringing these hidden characteristics into the light of our consciousness, we can weaken their negative influence on our behavior and prevent them from sabotaging our lives.

Exercise: Noticing Emotional Reactions

Emotional reactions are like our inner alarm system. They're our immediate responses when we're not thinking logically. It's crucial to pay attention to them because they carry vital information about our shadow.

In this exercise, start by noticing when you experience intense emotions. Look for patterns and try to identify what triggers these emotional reactions. Here are some questions to help you along the way.

> **Write down any specific words, actions, situations, or people that trigger your emotional reactions.**

_____

_____

_____

_____

_____

> **Jot down how you reacted physically and, more importantly, what feelings were driving those physical reactions.**

_____

_____

_____

_____

_____

As you think about why you felt that way, can you trace these feelings back to their origins? Write down what you uncover.

Once you've identified your triggers, or if you were already aware of them, you can move on to the next step. Now, this part can be a bit challenging. You need to be objective and dispassionate, which is easier said than done when you're feeling upset.

 While you are still feeling all those emotions and in that state of anger, fear, whatever that emotion is for you, write down your thoughts and feelings. Then, take a moment and step away until you've cooled down.

When you're ready, revisit your triggers and emotional reactions. Consider where these reactions originated. Here's the tough part: validate your feelings by acknowledging that, in the context of their origins, they might be rational. Then, calmly, logically, and reasonably, write about whether they're still rational in the context of what triggered them.

_____

_____

_____

_____

_____

By working through this exercise, you're beginning the journey of understanding and embracing your shadow self. Remember, it's all about self-discovery and self-compassion.

Where Does Shadow Work Come From?

I wanted to offer you five quick and intriguing facts about Jung and shadow work (Othon, 2017):

1 **Carl Jung's early passion:** Jung initially studied medicine but later followed his passion for understanding the human mind. He founded analytical psychology, which became the foundation for shadow work.

2 **The shadow metaphor:** Jung used the term "shadow" to describe the unconscious part of our minds, containing all the aspects of ourselves that we aren't aware of or choose to hide.

3 **Archetypes and symbols:** Jung believed that our unconscious minds contain universal symbols and archetypes that influence our thoughts, feelings, and behaviors. These archetypes are like primal blueprints for human experiences.

4 **Individuation process:** Jung believed that embracing our shadow selves is a crucial step in becoming our true selves. He called this process "individuation," where we integrate our hidden aspects to achieve wholeness.

5 **Influence on modern psychology:** Jung's ideas have had a profound impact on modern psychology, particularly in the realms of personality theory, dream analysis, and, of course, shadow work.

Jungian Archetypes-What Are They?

Now, let's take a closer look at Jungian archetypes. These are like the characters in the story of our lives, influencing how we think, feel, and act. Here's a brief description of a few key archetypes:

1. The Hero: The hero within us is courageous, determined, and always seeking adventure. They're driven by a desire to conquer challenges and make the world a better place.

2. The Shadow: As we're focusing on shadow work, it's important to mention this one. The Shadow represents the hidden, dark side of ourselves. It contains the aspects we've repressed or denied. Embracing the shadow is a central aspect of shadow work.

3. The Lover: The lover archetype is passionate, sensual, and seeks deep connections with others. It's the part of us that craves intimacy and meaningful relationships.

4. The Sage: The sage is wise, knowledgeable, and constantly seeking truth and understanding. It's the part of us that loves learning and seeks wisdom.

5. The Jester: This archetype is all about joy, humor, and living in the moment. The jester reminds us not to take life too seriously and to find laughter even in the darkest times.

Why Do I Need My Shadow Side?

You might be wondering why we should even bother with this shadow stuff. Well, it's essential, and here's why.

Remember, your shadow self is like a hidden room within you. It's where you've stashed away parts of yourself that you're not quite comfortable with or have been conditioned to reject. Despite being tucked away, this is still a part of who you are. This room may be filled with aspects that:

- **Scare us:** These are the facets of ourselves that send shivers down our spine. It could be the anger, jealousy, or vulnerability we'd rather not acknowledge.

- **Are linked to past trauma:** Sometimes, the shadow is intricately connected to painful memories from the past. These recollections can be like locked doors waiting to be opened.

- **Cause embarrassment, guilt, or shame:** We all have traits or actions that make us cringe with embarrassment or feel guilty and ashamed. These are often tucked away in the shadows, out of sight.

- **We don't want to face:** Confronting our shadow self can be daunting. It's like that cluttered closet we avoid, hoping it will magically tidy itself up.

I need you to try and understand that your shadow isn't all doom and gloom. In fact, it can hold things you've neglected. Perhaps you've always had an artistic soul but chose a "safe" career in accounting. Your creativity might be hidden away in that shadow room.

Sometimes, even positive traits end up in the shadows if they are dismissed or belittled by others. For instance, if someone told you that your sensitivity was a flaw, you might have buried it deep within.

Now, let's explore why it's so vital we embrace your shadow self:

- **Achieve personal growth:** When we confront our fears and limitations, we create room for personal growth. It's like nurturing a plant in the sunlight; you'll see it flourish.

- **Heal from past trauma:** Addressing past wounds may be painful, but it's a vital step in your healing journey. It's like cleaning out the dust and cobwebs in that hidden room.

- **Release guilt and shame:** Letting go of negative emotions tied to your shadow is incredibly liberating. It's like finally tossing out the old, worn-out items from that cluttered closet.

- **Reconnect with your true self:** Those positive traits and passions lurking in your shadow are part of your authentic self. Embracing them can bring you happiness and fulfillment that you didn't even know was possible.

You are not broken, weird, or odd for having a shadow self. Remember, we all have one, and it's an essential part of our human experience. Owning your shadow is an act of courage and self-love, a chance to reclaim those hidden parts of yourself that have been waiting for the light. There's a beautiful, authentic you waiting to be discovered in the shadows.

How Can Shadow Work Help?

I want you to imagine for a moment that you're trying to clean your room, but the lights are off. You stumble and trip over things, making little progress. To clean it thoroughly, you need to turn on the lights and see everything clearly. I mean true, actual spotlights shining into each and every corner of that room. You are finding things you haven't seen in years. The same principle applies to our inner world.

Shadow work is like turning on the lights in the room of your soul. It's about bringing to light those aspects of yourself that you've hidden away, often unconsciously. These hidden aspects, your "shadow," can include past traumas, unresolved emotions, and aspects of your personality you've deemed unacceptable. By shining a light on them, you can:

◆ **Heal:** Just as treating a wound requires cleaning it first, healing emotional wounds starts with acknowledging them. Shadow work helps you address and heal these emotional wounds.

◆ **Fully understand:** To understand yourself fully, you must explore every facet of your being, even the ones you've tucked away. In this life, we won't grow or heal if we only acknowledge the amazing things about ourselves. Shadow work provides you with the tools to do just that.

◆ **Improve:** Growth is impossible without self-awareness. Shadow work helps you become more aware of your patterns, triggers, and behaviors, enabling you to improve yourself and your life.

 ## Comparing the Pros and Cons of Shadow Work

Pros:

- **Personal growth:** Shadow work is a catalyst for profound personal growth, empowering you to become the best version of yourself.

- **Emotional liberation:** It frees you from the burden of repressed emotions, allowing you to experience emotional freedom. No more hiding behind those shadows.

- **Enhanced relationships:** As you better understand and heal yourself, your relationships can become healthier and more fulfilling.

Cons:

- **Emotional challenge:** Shadow work is emotionally challenging as you confront buried pain and emotions. We need to feel that pain before the light finds its way in.

- **Time-consuming:** It's a process that takes time and patience. Immediate results may not always be evident.

- **Requires self-compassion:** Self-compassion is essential because facing your shadows can trigger feelings of guilt or shame.

Dispelling common misconceptions about shadow work:

1 **It's only for "broken" people:** Shadow work is not just for those who are deeply wounded. It's a tool for anyone seeking personal growth and self-improvement.

2 **It's too dark and scary:** While it can be challenging, shadow work is a process of self-illumination, not darkness. It's about illuminating and bringing them a source of light.

3 **It's self-indulgent:** Shadow work is about self-awareness, not self-indulgence. It's a way to become a better person and improve your relationships.

4 **It's all about blame:** Shadow work is not about blaming yourself or others. It's about understanding and healing, not assigning blame.

5 **It's a one-time fix:** Shadow work is an ongoing process. It's not something you should expect to happen quickly but a healing journey of self-discovery and growth that lasts a lifetime.

Did you know that the word shadow work is trending on TikTok, with videos hitting 2.1 billion views and counting? Shadow work has gained TikTok traction, but we know it is nothing new. So, why the sudden gain in popularity? It is thought to have regained popularity because of a growing interest in overall self-awareness, holistic well-being, and personal growth (Mayer, 2023).

Be Mindful of the Triggers

We need to be mindful of why shadow work can be triggering. We also need to pay attention to how these emotional triggers are like neon lights pointing to areas in our lives that need our attention and care.

Let's begin by addressing a crucial aspect of shadow work—its potential to be triggering. When you start exploring your inner self, you might experience emotions and memories that you've long suppressed or ignored. This can feel uncomfortable and a bit scary at times. But remember, these emotional triggers are not obstacles; they are opportunities for healing.

- **Emotional triggers as neon lights:** Think of emotional triggers as red flags that signal unresolved issues within you. These triggers are like road signs, guiding you toward the areas in your life that need tender loving care. They point the way to hidden wounds that, once addressed, can lead to profound personal growth and emotional healing.

- **Keep track of your triggers:** As you continue down this path, keeping a journal or notebook handy is essential. Whenever you encounter an emotional trigger, take a moment to write it down. Describe the situation, your feelings, and any memories that surface. This will help you gain clarity on recurring patterns and themes in your life.

Exercise: Tracking Your Triggers

Let's dive into an exercise to help you identify and track your emotional triggers:

Step 1: Find a quiet and comfortable space where you won't be disturbed. Take a few deep breaths to center yourself.

Step 2: Below, notice the table with three columns: "Trigger," "Feelings," and "Memories."

Trigger	Feelings	Memories

Step 3: Whenever you encounter an emotional trigger in your daily life, write it down in the "Trigger" column. Be specific and honest about what triggered you.

Step 4: In the "Feelings" column, describe the emotions that arise when you're triggered. Are you angry, anxious, sad, or confused? Write it all down.

Step 5: In the "Memories" column, jot down any associated memories or past experiences that come to mind when you're triggered. These could be from your childhood, relationships, or other significant life events.

Step 6: After a week or two of tracking your triggers, take some time to review your entries. Notice any recurring patterns or themes. Are there specific triggers that keep resurfacing? Are there common feelings or memories associated with these triggers?

Step 7: Reflect on what you've discovered. What do these triggers tell you about yourself? How might they be connected to your past experiences or unresolved issues?

Remember, this exercise is about self-awareness, not judgment. It's a powerful tool to help you navigate your shadow with compassion and understanding. The more you become aware of your triggers, the better equipped you'll be to address them at your own pace.

I know we covered a lot of new territory and, at times, scary topics in this chapter. As I keep saying, we have to go into the dark before we find the light. It will be worth it you are worth it. In the next chapter, we will be leaning into our complete whole self. By becoming self-aware and acknowledging our suppressed emotions, limiting beliefs, and inner conflicts, we open the door to deep healing and personal growth. This chapter was meant to lay the foundation of shadow work, and now we will integrate our shadow self and uncover the hidden gems that reside within.

CHAPTER 2

SEEING THE SELF-

THE JOURNEY TO

SELF-ACCEPTANCE

Seeing the Self-
The Journey to Self-Acceptance

> *Your shadow is all of the things, 'positive' and 'negative,' that you've denied about yourself and hidden beneath the surface of the mask you forgot that you're wearing.* **–Oli Anderson**

If you're here, it means you've taken that courageous first step toward self-discovery and personal growth. I want you to know that I'm here to guide you through this process with compassion, understanding, and the utmost respect.

You may be feeling a mix of emotions right now—apprehension, curiosity, maybe even a bit of doubt. That's completely normal. Many of us, at some point in our lives, have felt like we're out of control, struggling to navigate the tumultuous sea of our own emotions. We've experienced anxiety, fear, guilt, sadness, exhaustion, and even depression. It's part of the human experience.

I want you to know that you have the power to regain control, to heal, and to find a path to emotional well-being. That's what shadow work is all about.

Seeing our entire being clearly helps us identify who we are, how we work best in life, and what we need to be successful. Imagine your self-awareness as a puzzle, and each piece of that puzzle represents a part of you. Some of those pieces may be shining in the light, while others are lurking in the shadows. The shadows are not something to be feared; they are simply parts of yourself that you haven't fully explored or accepted yet.

By obscuring part of our "picture," we limit our self-understanding and ability to grow and learn. Think of it as trying to drive a car with fogged-up windows—

you can only see part of the road, and that's a recipe for accidents. Shadow work is like clearing away the fog so you can navigate your life with clarity and purpose.

In this chapter, we're going to explore practical tips and strategies to help you become more self-aware of the full self. You'll discover how to shine a light on those hidden parts of you so you can embrace them and use them to your advantage.

We'll also delve into relevant research and studies that support the concepts we discuss, giving you a solid foundation to understand why shadow work is so valuable. And, to make it all the more relatable, I'll share stories and case studies from real people who've embarked on their journey of self-discovery and transformation.

Remember, you have within you the potential for profound growth and healing. So, take a deep breath, let go of any apprehension, and let's start this transformative journey together. The destination? A more self-aware, self-accepting, and empowered you.

Are you ready? Let's begin.

Stories of Self-Awareness

The Lion Who Thought He Was a Sheep

Once upon a time, in a vast field, a lioness was nearing the end of her life. Tragically, she passed away shortly after giving birth to a cub. Confused and alone, the newborn lion cub found itself amidst a herd of sheep. A mother sheep took pity on the cub and decided to raise it as one of her own.

As the days turned into months, the lion cub grew up alongside the sheep. It adapted to their ways, bleating like a sheep and munching on grass. Yet, deep inside, it always felt like something was missing. The other sheep, in their ignorance, would often taunt the young lion, saying, "You're so odd! Your voice is strange. Why can't you be like the rest of us? You don't belong here!"

The lion endured the ridicule silently, feeling like it had betrayed the sheep community by being different. One day, an older lion from a distant jungle spotted the herd of sheep and decided to attack. Mid-chase, the older lion noticed the young lion running with the sheep.

Curiosity got the better of him, and he abandoned the chase, focusing on the younger lion instead. Pouncing on the cub, he growled, "Why are you running with these sheep?"

Terrified, the young lion stammered, "Please don't eat me! I'm just a sheep, I promise!"

The older lion, however, insisted, "That's not true! You are not a sheep; you are a lion, just like me."

The young lion repeated, "I'm a sheep please let me go."

The older lion had an idea. He dragged the young lion to a nearby river and urged it to look at its reflection. To its astonishment, the young lion saw its true self—a magnificent lion, not a sheep. Overwhelmed with joy, it roared mightily. The roar echoed through the jungle, frightening the sheep hiding in the bushes. They scattered, unable to mock or be near the lion anymore.

 ## *Moral of the Story*

The older lion represents self-awareness, and the reflection in the water symbolizes self-reflection. Just like the young lion, you may have grown up in a negative environment, absorbing limiting beliefs. But by looking inward, becoming self-aware, and challenging those beliefs, you can discover your true nature and align your life with it.

The older lion is not external but resides within you—it's your true self, your awareness. Let your awareness shine a light on your limiting beliefs, and you'll find your authentic self. Don't let past influences keep you stuck in your current reality; focus on self-discovery and growth.

Taming the Quick Temper

In a peaceful village, a young man approached a wise Zen master, seeking help for his uncontrollable anger. "My quick temper is ruining my relationships," he confessed.

The Zen master offered assistance, saying, "Can you show me your anger?"

The young man replied, "It happens suddenly; I can't demonstrate it right now."

The Zen master gently questioned, "If it's not present all the time, is it truly a part of your nature? Something that comes and goes isn't your true self, and you need not be defined by it."

The young man pondered this wisdom and left. As time passed, he began to observe his temper more closely. He gained control over it by bringing conscious awareness to it and repairing his damaged relationships.

 ## Moral of the Story

Your emotions don't define you, but they can control you if left unchecked. The path to taming subconscious reactions is to bring conscious awareness to them. Once you shine the light of consciousness on a belief, action, or emotion, it loses its power over you.

The Importance of Embracing the Light

So, why is it essential to embrace both the light and the shadow sides of ourselves? Let me explain with a real-life scenario:

Think of shadow work as a way to shed light on the hidden aspects of your inner world. The parts that often stay in the shadows are the emotions, thoughts, and experiences we've been told are wrong or unacceptable. For example, consider someone who firmly believes that feeling resentment as a father means they're ungrateful or a bad dad.

When this father has anger or frustration toward his child or a challenging situation in their life, they might react by ignoring or denying those feelings. They might even start thinking less of themselves because of these emotions. It's something many of us can relate to—feeling like we're not allowed to have certain feelings. "I better suppress this feeling, or I will be seen as this horrible dad."

These messages about what's acceptable and what's not come from various sources—our parents, relatives, teachers, and society at large. The problem is anything deemed "unacceptable" gets pushed into the shadow, hidden away from our conscious awareness.

By working on accepting and integrating these shadowed thoughts and emotions, we can experience greater internal peace. Instead of being driven unconsciously by our shadow self's hidden needs and feelings, we gain control over our reactions and emotions.

Embracing both the light and the shadow aspects of ourselves is an essential part of personal growth and self-awareness. Here's why we need it:

◆ **Wholeness and balance:** Each individual has positive and negative aspects of their personality, emotions, and experiences. Ignoring or repressing the shadow side can lead to an imbalance in your psyche. Embracing both sides allows you to become a more whole and balanced person.

◆ **Self-acceptance:** You can practice self-compassion and self-acceptance by acknowledging and accepting your shadow aspects. It's a way of saying, "I am human, and I have flaws and imperfections, but I am still deserving of love and respect."

◆ **Healing and growth:** Shadow work involves exploring your past wounds, traumas, fears, and negative patterns of behavior. By delving into these aspects of yourself, you can heal old wounds and grow as a person. It's a way to discover more about yourself and find ways to improve.

◆ **Improved relationships:** Understanding your own shadows can also help you better understand and navigate your interactions with others. It can lead to more empathetic and compassionate relationships because you're less likely to project your own unresolved issues onto others.

◆ **Increased self-awareness:** Shadow work fosters self-awareness by bringing unconscious patterns and behaviors to the surface. This awareness allows you to make conscious choices rather than reacting unconsciously to triggers from your shadow self.

◆ **Spiritual growth:** For some, embracing the shadow is a spiritual practice. It's seen as a path to enlightenment and self-realization, as it encourages self-examination and the pursuit of inner truth.

◆ **Creativity and authenticity:** Embracing your shadow can unlock hidden creative potentials and allow you to express yourself more authentically. Often, our most profound art, writing, and ideas come from our darkest and most vulnerable places.

So what happens if you never look into your shadows? That's a great question. Here are several things that can happen:

◆ **Unconscious patterns persist:** Unexamined shadows can continue to influence your behavior, often in destructive or self-sabotaging ways. You may repeatedly find yourself in unhealthy relationships or situations without understanding why.

◆ **Repression and denial:** Repressing your shadow aspects can lead to psychological and emotional problems. It's like sweeping issues under the rug instead of addressing them head-on.

◆ **Stagnation:** Without shadow work, personal growth and self-awareness can stagnate. You may miss out on opportunities for healing, transformation, and a deeper understanding of yourself.

◆ **Projection onto others:** Unresolved shadow aspects can lead to projecting your own negative qualities onto others. This can harm relationships and prevent you from taking responsibility for your own actions and feelings.

Embracing the light and the shadow of ourselves is key to personal growth, self-awareness, and overall well-being. It's a journey toward becoming a more balanced, authentic, and compassionate individual. Shadow work is a valuable tool in this process, helping you confront and integrate the hidden aspects of your psyche.

What Feeds Our Shadow Self?

Essentially, six key things feed our shadow self. Let's take a few moments and explore those more closely.

 ## *Avoidance*

Imagine you have a messy room in your house that you don't like to enter. You keep the door closed and avoid going in there because it's uncomfortable and chaotic. Similarly, avoidance in shadow work is when we dodge, ignore, or run away from parts of ourselves that make us uncomfortable. These can be feelings, memories, or thoughts we don't want to deal with. But guess what? The more we avoid them, the more they grow in the shadows.

 ## *Suppression*

Think of suppression like pushing a beachball underwater. You're using a lot of energy to keep it down, but eventually, it pops back up when you're not expecting it. In shadow work, suppression happens when we try to hide or bury parts of ourselves because we're afraid others won't accept them. This often comes from society's rules, like how we should behave, look, or think. We hide our true feelings and opinions to fit in, but this keeps our shadow self hidden and powerful.

Social Expectations and Suppression

Imagine you're in a group of friends who all like a certain type of music. You might pretend to like that music too, even if you don't really enjoy it, just to fit in. This is because social norms and what our group considers normal can pressure us to hide our true preferences, opinions, or quirks. We suppress our uniqueness to belong.

 ## *Denial*

Denial is like pretending that a big problem isn't there. It's like saying, "I'm not feeling sad at all," when you're actually bursting with sadness. In shadow work, denial is when we refuse to accept our flaws, mistakes, or negative feelings. We might say, "I'm always fine," even when we're hurting inside. Denial keeps us from recognizing and working on the parts of ourselves that need healing.

 ## *Guilt and Shame*

Imagine carrying around a heavy backpack filled with rocks. Guilt and shame are like those heavy rocks. Guilt is feeling bad about something you did, while shame is feeling like you're a bad person because of it. When we carry guilt and shame, we're feeding our shadow self. These emotions can make us hide our actions and emotions, trapping us in the shadows.

 ## *Fear*

Think of fear as a big, scary monster under your bed. It's the feeling that something bad will happen if you show your true self. Fear stops us from taking risks, expressing our needs, or being vulnerable. It's like a guard at the entrance to our shadow self, preventing us from exploring and understanding it.

Exercise: Getting to Know Your Shadow Self

Let's do a simple exercise to help you identify with your shadow self.

Find a quiet, comfortable, safe space.

Take a few deep breaths to relax.

 Write down any memories, feelings, or thoughts you've been avoiding, suppressing, denying, feeling guilty or shameful about, or are afraid to face. Be honest with yourself. Remember, there's no judgment here; it's just you exploring your own feelings and experiences.

_____

_____

_____

_____

_____

_____

_____

After you've done this, take 24 hours to reflect on what you've jotted down.

Now, revisit what you wrote and reflect. Write down how they make you feel. Are you more comfortable with these emotions now than when you first wrote them? Can you feel a shift? These are the aspects of your shadow self, and acknowledging them is the first step to understanding and healing.

_____

_____

_____

_____

_____

_____

_____

_____

_____

_____

This exercise is like grabbing that flashing light and shining it into all those spaces in the attic and basement we've been avoiding. It may feel uncomfortable at first, but it's the beginning of your journey to embrace and befriend your shadow self. Remember, you're not alone in this, and you have the power to bring light to your shadows for personal growth and healing.

Embracing Our Whole Self

Before we dive into the "how," let's explore the "why." Why is it essential to embrace all facets of yourself, even the ones deemed to be lurking in the shadows? Well, here's the truth: we are complex beings, a kaleidoscope of experiences, emotions, and memories. Ignoring or suppressing parts of ourselves can lead to a whirlwind of unwanted feelings like anxiety, fear, guilt, sadness, and even depression.

Think of your shadow self as the unsung hero of your story. These hidden aspects hold the key to your growth, resilience, and healing. By acknowledging and accepting them, you not only free yourself from their grip but also pave the way for a more balanced, authentic, and joyful life.

 ## *How to Accept Ourselves*

Acceptance is a big deal in shadow work. It is easy to love and accept all the ooey, gooey pieces of ourselves. Learning to accept each and every detail is how we find absolute peace and growth. Let's review a few ways to find acceptance with our whole self.

Practice Self-Compassion

Begin by treating yourself with the same kindness and understanding you'd offer a dear friend. Recognize that you're human and that making mistakes is a part of life.

Journal Your Thoughts

Feel free to use the space below to jot down your thoughts and feelings. This can help you gain clarity about your emotions and enable you to observe them from a more detached perspective. What should you focus on? Great question. I went ahead and added journal prompts to help.

 List at least five strengths, talents, or qualities you appreciate about yourself. How have these strengths positively impacted your life?

Your Strengths & Talents	Impact on Your Life
1. _____	1. _____
2. _____	2. _____
3. _____	3. _____
4. _____	4. _____
5. _____	5. _____

Write down a few of your perceived flaws or imperfections. Now, challenge yourself to see if there's a positive aspect or hidden strength within each of them.

Perceived Flaws	Hidden Strengths Within Your Flaws
1. _____	1. _____
2. _____	2. _____
3. _____	3. _____
4. _____	4. _____
5. _____	5. _____

 Describe a recent situation where you were hard on yourself. How could you have shown more self-compassion in that moment? What would you say to a friend who was in a similar situation?

_____

_____

_____

_____

Reflect on a mistake or regret from your past that you struggle to accept. Write about what you've learned from that experience and how it has shaped you.

_____

_____

_____

_____

_____

_____

Imagine a version of yourself who is unconditionally loved and accepted just as they are. Describe this version of yourself in detail. What would change in your life if you treated yourself with such love and acceptance?

_____

_____

_____

_____

_____

Identify and describe your inner critic—the voice inside that judges and criticizes you. What triggers your inner critic, and how can you respond to it with kindness and understanding?

_____

_____

_____

_____

_____

 What are some specific actions or steps you can take to practice self-acceptance daily? Set achievable goals for yourself.

1. _____

2. _____

3. _____

4. _____

5. _____

6. _____

7. _____

8. _____

Think of someone you admire and believe embodies self-acceptance. What qualities or behaviors do they exhibit that you could incorporate into your own life?

1. _____

2. _____

3. _____

4. _____

5. _____

6. _____

7. _____

8. _____

Write a letter to your future self, expressing your hopes for continued growth, self-acceptance, and self-love. What advice would you give your future self?

Date: -   -

_____,

_____

_____

_____

_____

_____

_____

_____

_____

_____

_____

_____

_____

_____

How to Forgive Ourselves

Forgiving ourselves can be challenging, especially when we carry the weight of past mistakes. But remember, forgiving doesn't mean condoning the actions; it means releasing yourself from their grip. Try this forgiveness exercise:

 ### *Exercise: Letter to Yourself*

Find a quiet space where you won't be disturbed.

 Use the space below to write a letter to yourself, addressing the issue or mistake you want to forgive. Express your feelings honestly. Share your pain, anger, or disappointment.

_____,

_____

_____

_____

_____

_____

_____

_____

_____

_____

_____

Now, shift your focus toward self-compassion. Remind yourself that you are human and humans make mistakes. It's a part of our journey.

 In the space below, write a forgiveness statement: "I forgive myself for [specific mistake]. I release myself from its burden." Close the letter with words of self-love and acceptance.

I forgive myself for

_____

_____

_____

_____

_____

I release myself from it's burden and

_____

_____

_____

_____

_____

_____

Read this letter to yourself aloud. Feel the weight lifting as you say those forgiving words.

Embracing all parts of yourself, even the shadowy ones, is a powerful step toward healing and living a more fulfilled life. Keep going, and know that you're not alone on this path.

Exercise: Exploring Your Emotional Patterns

 List the emotions you experience most frequently (e.g., anxiety, fear, guilt). Now, next to each emotion, write down situations or triggers that typically evoke these feelings.

Emotions	What Evoked that Emotion?
1. _____	1. _____
2. _____	2. _____
3. _____	3. _____
4. _____	4. _____
5. _____	5. _____

Reflect on any recurring themes or patterns you notice. Is there a common thread connecting these emotions?

_____

_____

_____

_____

Ask yourself why you feel this way in those situations. What beliefs or past experiences might be contributing to these emotions?

Don't judge yourself during this activity. The goal is simply to become more aware of your emotional landscape.

Mindfulness Is the Key

Mindfulness is a powerful tool in the realm of shadow work. It helps us transcend the ego, uncover our shadows, and heal from past traumas, all while getting in touch with our true selves. Let's explore mindfulness for self-awareness and ways to incorporate it into your daily life.

Mindfulness is a wonderful tool that lets us observe our thoughts, physical sensations, and emotions without judgment. This non-judgmental awareness is vital in shadow work because it helps us uncover hidden aspects of ourselves. When we're mindful, we can explore our shadow without being overwhelmed by it or reacting defensively.

How to Be More Mindful

- **Meditation:** It's like going to the gym for your mind. It strengthens your ability to be present and aware. It's a cornerstone of mindfulness because it teaches you to observe your thoughts and feelings without attachment. There are three types of meditation:

  - ◊ **Breathing and counting:** Find a quiet space, sit comfortably, and focus on your breath. Inhale deeply, counting to four, then exhale, counting to four. When your mind wanders (and it will), gently bring your attention back to your breath.

  - ◊ **Body scan:** Lie down or sit comfortably and bring your attention to different parts of your body, starting from your toes and moving up to your head. Be mindful of any sensations or feelings without trying to change them.

  - ◊ **Walking meditation:** Take a slow, deliberate walk. Pay attention to the sensation of your feet lifting, moving, and landing. Feel the ground beneath you with each step.

- **Using your senses:** Take a moment to pause during your day and engage your senses. For example, while having a meal, really taste the flavors, smell the aromas, and feel the textures. Doing this will help keep you present.

- **Notice your thoughts and feelings:** Imagine your thoughts and feelings as clouds passing by in the sky. Instead of getting carried away by them, stand back and observe them. Ask yourself, "What am I thinking and feeling right now?" without judgment.

How to Include Mindfulness in Your Daily Life

Okay, so we now know that being mindful is important, but as busy as we are, how can we possibly fit it into our day? Below, you will find some helpful suggestions to do just that:

- **Morning routine:** Start your day with a short mindfulness practice, even if it's just a few minutes of deep breathing or a quick body scan.

- **Mindful breaks:** Take short mindfulness breaks throughout the day. Set reminders on your phone to pause, breathe deeply, and notice your surroundings.

- **Mindful eating:** You can achieve this by enjoying each bite before swallowing. Focus on those amazing flavors in your mouth. Put away distractions like phones or TV and fully engage with your meal.

- **Mindful walking:** Incorporate mindfulness into your daily walks. Pay attention to the rhythm of your steps and the world around you.

Now, whenever you need an instant dose of mindfulness, simply:

- **Pause:** Simply pause what you're doing.

- **Breathe:** Take a few deep breaths to center yourself.

- **Observe:** Notice your thoughts, emotions, and physical sensations in the moment.

Remember, mindfulness is a skill that improves with practice. Be patient with yourself and approach it with an open heart. Over time, it will become an essential tool in your shadow work journey, helping you connect with your true self and heal from past wounds.

In this chapter, we've explored the profound power of mindfulness in peeling back the layers of your true self, moving beyond the ego, shadow, and trauma. You've learned that by being mindful, you can observe your thoughts, feelings, and sensations without judgment, creating a deeper connection with your authentic self.

In the upcoming chapter, you will check out practical guidance, exercises, and safety measures to ensure that you embark on this path with confidence and care. I understand that this can be a vulnerable process, and your well-being is always the utmost priority. So, get ready to explore your inner world further, heal old wounds, and discover the incredible potential that lies within you.

CHAPTER 3
SAFE INWARD
JOURNEYS

Safe Inward Journeys

> *It is only through shadows that one comes to know the light. –*
> ***St. Catherine of Siena***

During this chapter, I want to spend some time examining the essential art of creating safe spaces within ourselves for the profound work that lies ahead. If you're new to shadow work, you might be feeling a mix of curiosity and apprehension.

We'll explore the importance of safety in the inward journey. Just as an explorer prepares for an expedition with the right gear and knowledge, we must prepare ourselves for the expedition into our inner world. I want to equip you with the tools, techniques, and understanding needed to ensure your journey is as safe and nurturing as possible.

Before we dive into practical tips and transformative activities, let's address why this chapter is so important.

You may have noticed that you're experiencing a range of challenging emotions–anxiety, fear, guilt, sadness, and exhaustion. You might even be dealing with depression. These feelings are signs that you're carrying a heavy emotional burden, a part of which is hidden in your shadow self. It's natural to want to explore and heal these wounds, but doing so without proper preparation can sometimes lead to emotional overwhelm.

Think of shadow work as an archeological dig into the depths of your psyche. As you unearth long-buried emotions and beliefs, you might encounter treasures of self-awareness, but you might also stumble upon hidden pain and trauma. That's why it's crucial to create a safe environment within yourself–a sanctuary where you can explore without feeling overwhelmed or unsafe.

What to Expect in This Chapter

◆ **Practical tips and strategies:** I'll provide you with easy-to-follow guidelines on how to establish a personal, mental, and emotional safe space. These strategies will help you navigate the often challenging terrain of your inner world.

◆ **Workbook activities:** Throughout this chapter, you'll find interactive exercises designed to help you apply the concepts we discuss. These activities are like the tools you'll need for your inward journey, helping you dig deeper and uncover the hidden gems within your shadow self.

◆ **Research and studies:** I'll present you with insights from psychological research and studies related to self-guided therapy and shadow work. This knowledge will give you a solid foundation as you embark on your exploration.

◆ **Relatable stories:** To remind you that you're not alone on this journey, I'll share stories and case studies of individuals who have walked a similar path. These stories will provide inspiration and show you that transformation is possible.

As we move forward, remember that shadow work is a profound act of self-love and personal growth. The road may be challenging, but it's also incredibly rewarding. Our goal is to create a safe and inviting space for you to explore your inner world, gain self-understanding, and embark on a healing journey that can transform your life.

So, let's begin. Let's be safe, compassionate, and resilient!

Morgan's Story

Morgan had carried the weight of anxiety and self-doubt for as long as she could remember. She often found herself stuck in a cycle of self-criticism, unable to break free from the grip of her inner demons. One day, while browsing through a local bookstore, she stumbled upon a book about shadow work. It was a serendipitous moment, one that would change the course of her life.

Morgan's anxiety was like a persistent shadow, always lurking in the background. It kept her from pursuing her dreams, forming meaningful connections, and feeling at ease in her own skin. She knew she needed to confront these inner demons to find true happiness and fulfillment.

With a mix of apprehension and determination, Morgan decided to delve into the world of shadow work. She began by setting aside a small corner of her cozy apartment, a safe space for her journey of self-discovery. Armed with a journal and a commitment to herself, she started writing down her thoughts and feelings.

Each evening, Morgan would sit in her favorite armchair, pen in hand, and pour her heart onto the pages of her journal. She wrote about her fears, her past traumas, and her insecurities. At first, it was painful to confront these aspects of herself, but gradually, she began to see patterns emerge. The act of writing allowed her to distance herself from her emotions to observe them from a more objective standpoint.

In addition to journaling, Morgan embraced meditation as a way to quiet her racing thoughts. She would sit on her balcony, surrounded by the gentle rustling of leaves, and focus on her breath. This practice brought her a newfound sense of calm and allowed her to connect with her inner self.

Recognizing the importance of community, Morgan sought out support groups for people on their own shadow work journeys. Here, she found kindred spirits who shared their stories and provided guidance. Being part of a group gave her a sense of belonging and reassurance that she wasn't alone in her struggles.

As Morgan continued her self-guided self-help journey, she experienced moments of breakthrough and liberation. She uncovered the root causes of her anxiety and self-doubt, often tied to childhood experiences and societal pressures. Understanding these origins was like turning on a light in the darkness of her mind.

Yet, there came a time when Morgan's anxiety became overwhelming. It was during a particularly challenging week when she decided to take a step further. She reached out to those she trusted; she didn't try to go it alone. She also was mindful of those times when she would need to lean on her therapist. Understanding that took a burden off her own shoulders. She felt more comfortable continuing her work, knowing the help was there when and if she needed it.

Morgan combined the insights she gained from self-help with the expertise of her therapist. Together, they created a well-rounded approach to her healing journey. Morgan continued her journaling and meditation.

Morgan's journey was messy and wonderful, and it was also transformative. Over time, her anxiety and self-doubt gradually loosened their grip on her. She learned to be kinder to herself, to accept her imperfections, and to embrace her shadow as an integral part of who she was.

Morgan's story is a testament to the power of self-guided self-help, combined with the wisdom of professional guidance when needed. It's proof that, with courage and commitment, anyone can embark on a journey of self-discovery, healing, and personal growth. Morgan's life transformed, and yours can, too, as you venture into your own shadow work journey.

Remember, you have the power within you to explore and heal your shadow self. Self-guided self-help is a valuable tool to get you started on this path, but don't hesitate to seek professional help when needed.

Exercise: Journaling for Insecurities

I want to take a pause here and ask you to do some shadow work. In the space below, I would like you to do some journaling. Much like in Morgan's story above, journaling can help you focus on your insecurities, fears, and past trauma.

Before diving into these questions, remember that shadow work can be emotionally challenging. Find a time when you have solitude and can devote your full attention to these reflections. Feel free to select and modify the prompts that resonate most with you and answer those for the most effective results.

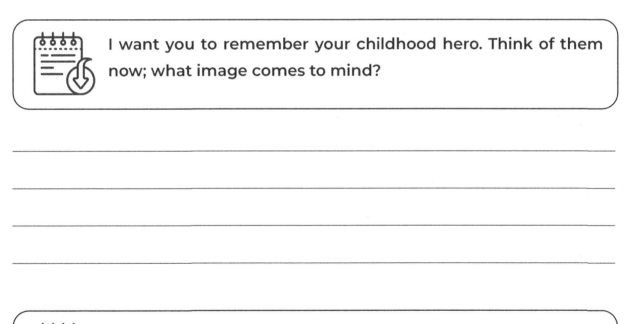

I want you to remember your childhood hero. Think of them now; what image comes to mind?

_____

_____

_____

_____

 When was the first time you felt insecure as a child? Do you remember what triggered this feeling?

_____

_____

_____

As a child, when did you first feel let down? Write down as many details surrounding the circumstances. Do you feel this affected your ability to accept help and love? How?

_____

_____

_____

_____

Recall your parents' or guardians' beliefs during your childhood. Are your current beliefs aligned with theirs? How are you different? How are you the same?

_____

_____

_____

Think back to beliefs you were made to follow in your childhood that you now resent as an adult. Do these influence your behavior today? How?

_____

_____

_____

When you find yourself feeling insecure, do you participate in self-sabotaging actions? If so, which ones?

1. _____

2. _____

3. _____

4. _____

5. _____

Can you think of any beliefs from your childhood that contribute to your insecurity? For instance, thoughts like "This is too difficult" or "I'm not good enough."

1. _____
_____

2. _____
_____

3. _____
_____

4. _____
_____

5. _____
_____

Do you think your insecurities hold you back? If so, explain how.

_____

_____

_____

_____

_____

_____

How do social media, parental pressures, or even cultural expectations cause insecurity in you?

_____

_____

_____

_____

_____

_____

Do you have difficulty not comparing yourself to others? Why do you think you do this?

_____

_____

_____

_____

_____

_____

Take your time with these questions, and remember that the process is about self-discovery and growth. Embrace each insight as a step toward a more profound understanding of yourself and your journey toward healing and personal development.

Can You Really Be Your Own Therapist?

While professional therapy has its benefits, self-guided self-help is a fantastic complement or even a starting point, especially if you're on a budget or want to explore your inner world at your own pace.

I want to emphasize that self-guided self-help is not a replacement for professional therapy, especially if you're dealing with severe emotional issues. However, it can be a powerful supplement to your healing journey. Here are some tips on how to effectively become your own self-therapist:

- **Read and research widely:**

  Educate yourself about shadow work, self-awareness, and personal growth. Books, articles, and online resources can provide valuable insights and guidance.

- **Attend workshops and support groups:**

  If possible, participate in local workshops or online support groups. Connecting with others on a similar journey can be incredibly enriching.

- **One thing at a time:**

  Avoid overwhelming yourself by trying to tackle all your issues simultaneously. Choose one aspect of your shadow self to focus on at a time.

- **Journal, but don't ruminate:**

  Give yourself time each day for journaling and self-reflection. This helps you process your thoughts and emotions without dwelling on them throughout the day.

- **Get other perspectives:**

  Seek out trusted friends, mentors, or support groups to gain different viewpoints on your challenges. An outside perspective often provides clarity.

- **Use talk as therapy with a trusted mentor or friend:**

  Engage in open and honest conversations with someone you trust. Sharing your feelings and thoughts can be therapeutic in itself.

- **Be mindful:**

  Mindfulness practices, such as meditation and deep breathing, can help you become more aware of your emotions and reactions.

- **Do check in with a counselor, mentor, life coach, or friend if needed:**

  Recognize when self-help isn't enough. If your emotions become too overwhelming or if you feel stuck, it's perfectly okay to seek professional guidance.

Studies have shown that people who actively engage in self-help practices often experience improved emotional regulation, increased self-awareness, and enhanced overall well-being (Ackerman, 2019). While self-help is a valuable tool, it's essential to remember that it may not be sufficient for everyone, particularly those with complex emotional challenges.

The Affordability and Accessibility of Self-Guided Therapy

We need to address the elephant in the room—the affordability and accessibility of therapy. It's a very real issue that many people face, and it can indeed create anxiety and uncertainty.

So, picture this: a recent survey of 1000 adults in therapy across America came up with some interesting findings. Nearly 40% of the folks in the survey had to reach out for some financial assistance just to make it to their therapy sessions. Among the survey participants, a majority (that's 62%) mentioned that they had to dig into their own pockets for some therapy expenses. On average, that came up to about $178 a month, even though a whopping 71% said they had some insurance coverage, and 36% were getting a hand from Employee Assistance Programs (EAP) to help with the costs (Ingram, 2022).

Now, here's where it gets real. A significant chunk, about 38%, needed some financial support from someone else just to keep up with therapy. And for some, the financial strain was so heavy that they had to hit pause on their therapy sessions. Roughly a third had to cancel appointments because of those out-of-pocket costs, 39% cut back on the frequency of their sessions to save some cash, and 31% temporarily stopped therapy to manage bigger expenses. Over 1 in 3 Americans surveyed who are no longer in therapy shared that they had to quit because of cost-related reasons (Ingram, 2022).

So, you see, the need for therapy is on the rise, but the worry about being able to afford it isn't going away. This is where self-guided therapy steps in as an accessible and cost-effective option to help you on your journey to personal growth and healing.

Let's break down why self-guided therapy can be beneficial:

- **Cost-effective:** Self-guided therapy is budget-friendly. In fact, it's often significantly more affordable than traditional therapy sessions. You won't have to worry about recurring out-of-pocket expenses, like co-pays or monthly fees. You can access self-guided resources for a fraction of the cost and sometimes even for free.

- **No insurance hassles:** You won't have to navigate the complexities of insurance coverage or worry about insurance changes affecting your access to therapy. Self-guided therapy puts you in control of your healing journey without financial constraints.

- **Flexible schedule:** Self-guided therapy allows you to work at your own pace and on your own schedule. This flexibility is especially beneficial if you have a busy life or commitments that make it challenging to attend regular therapy appointments.

- **Privacy and comfort:** You get to create a safe and inviting space for yourself to explore your shadow self. There's no need to share your innermost thoughts and feelings with a stranger. Self-guided therapy allows you to reflect and grow in the comfort of your own space.

- **Consistent progress:** With self-guided therapy, you can maintain a consistent practice without worrying about financial setbacks. This consistency can lead to more significant personal growth and self-healing over time.

- **Evidence-based approaches:** Self-guided therapy often incorporates research-based strategies and techniques, ensuring that you receive effective guidance in your journey toward self-awareness and healing.

We love and value therapists. The work they do is invaluable, and there are specific roles they play in the mental health field. It is essential to understand that. It is also important to know what role you can play in your mental health journey.

Self-guided therapy provides an affordable, accessible, and effective way to explore your shadow self, regulate your emotions, and experience personal growth. It's a valuable option to consider on your path to self-healing, offering you the tools and resources to take control of your emotional well-being without the financial burden.

Tracking Your Progress

I know that shadow work can be a challenging yet profoundly rewarding endeavor. As you embark on this path toward understanding your shadow self, tracking your progress is an essential compass guiding you through the twists and turns of your inner landscape. Here, I'll provide you with practical tips and exercises to help you do just that.

 ## *Exercise: Journaling Your Progress*

I recommend the tactile approach of writing down your answers as it engages a different part of your brain, fostering deeper reflection and growth. Now, let's get started:

 Before diving into shadow work, take a moment to reflect on where you are right now. Write down your current emotional state, thoughts, and any specific challenges you're facing. Be honest with yourself; this is your starting point, your reference for measuring progress.

_____

_____

_____

_____

_____

_____

_____

_____

_____

> Establishing achievable goals is like setting the destination on your GPS for this journey. What are you looking to achieve through shadow work? Write down your goals, needs, and desires. Remember, effective goals should be specific, measurable, achievable, and flexible. For instance, if you're working on why certain people trigger you, your goal could be to be kinder and more respectful to people, regardless of who they are.

_____

_____

_____

_____

_____

_____

Tracking your progress involves understanding your emotional landscape. Create a daily routine where you check in with your feelings. Use a simple chart to jot down how you're feeling when you wake up, and note if it changes throughout the day. Ask yourself why your emotions fluctuate. If something significant happens during the day that affects your feelings, make a note of it.

Here's a sample chart:

DAY 1

Morning Emotion: _____

_____

_____

_____

_____

Evening Emotion: _____

_____

_____

_____

_____

What changed today: _____

_____

_____

_____

_____

DAY 2

Morning Emotion: _____

_____

_____

_____

_____

Evening Emotion: _____

_____

_____

_____

_____

What changed today: _____

_____

_____

_____

_____

DAY 3

Morning Emotion: _____

_____

_____

_____

_____

Evening Emotion: _____

_____

_____

_____

_____

What changed today: _____

_____

_____

_____

_____

Throughout your journey, pay close attention to any shifts or changes in how you feel. Write them down. Are you noticing improvements in your mood, confidence, or overall outlook on life? Conversely, are there recurring themes or triggers that still cause you distress? Actively recognizing these changes will help tailor your shadow work plan to meet your evolving needs.

List Your Improvements	Triggers Still Causing You Distress

Remember that progress takes various forms. It might be a sense of relief after a challenging session, feeling more in control of your emotions, or witnessing changes in your behavior and thought patterns. These changes may be subtle, so keep an eye out for them.

Sometimes, those close to us can spot our progress before we do. Don't hesitate to seek feedback and insight from trusted friends, family members, or support groups. Their external perspective can provide a more comprehensive picture of your growth.

Maintain open and honest communication with yourself. This is key to tracking your progress. Write down your experiences, challenges, and victories openly and regularly. Be open; nobody else will read this. This practice will help you monitor your progress over time and identify any challenges hindering your growth. Even when facing setbacks, be honest with yourself and record them. Setbacks are part of the journey, not a roadblock.

Lastly, consider keeping a dedicated journal or note-taking app for your shadow work. This will serve as a valuable reference for reflecting on your progress. Jot down your thoughts, emotions, breakthroughs, and setbacks. It's like keeping a diary of your inner transformation, and it can help you stay organized and gain insights into your journey.

Remember, tracking your progress is not about judgment; it's about self-discovery and growth. Celebrate each and every one of your successes, and acknowledge your challenges as stepping stones toward a better you. With each step, you're closer to understanding and owning your shadow self.

What If I Need Help?

Rest assured that there is a good chance you will. I don't say this to frighten you but only to prepare you. Laying all the cards on the table allows one to know what to expect and educate themselves. So, when the time comes, and you feel that overwhelming need for backup, what should you do?

First, I want to remind you to take your time. It is far too common in traditional therapy that we complain about how long it is taking. That is for a reason. If we rush certain processes, we can do more harm than good. Take your time, and progress at a pace that feels comfortable for you. If you feel overwhelmed or like you're moving too quickly, it's okay to slow down. This is your journey, and you must honor your timing.

 ## *Have a Support Shadow Work Buddy*

Now, let's say you are going about your process at a reasonable pace, yet you still feel those feelings of anxiety or fear rushing in. It can be incredibly beneficial to have a partner or friend who is also on a path of self-discovery. This person can be your sounding board, someone to bounce ideas off of, and a source of encouragement when things get tough. Together, you can share your experiences, learn from each other, and provide emotional support during challenging moments.

 ## *Use Self-Calming and Self-Soothing Techniques*

There will be times when you encounter intense emotions or challenging aspects of yourself during shadow work. During these moments, it's crucial to have tools at your disposal to calm and soothe yourself. Here are some techniques to try:

Grounding Exercises

- **5-4-3-2-1 grounding:** This is a common exercise to keep you present and calm. Start with calling out five things you can physically see. Then, move on to four things you can actually touch. Next are three things you can hear and two things you can smell in the air. Last, you want to focus on one thing you can taste, for instance, maybe that lingering coffee you just had. This exercise helps bring you back to the present moment.

- **Rooted visualization:** Imagine yourself as a tree with deep roots firmly planted in the earth. Feel the stability and support of the ground beneath you.

- **Deep breathing:** Take slow, deep breaths, focusing on the sensation of your breath moving in and out. This helps calm your nervous system.

- **Body scan:** Mentally scan your body, starting from your toes and moving up to your head. Pay attention to any areas of tension and consciously release it.

- **Nature connection:** Spend time in nature, whether it's a walk in the park or sitting in your backyard. Nature has a calming effect on our emotions.

 # Calming Exercises

- **Progressive muscle relaxation:** For this exercise, you are going to start at the very top of your head and work down to your toes. Working one muscle group at a time, you want to tense that muscle group, for instance, your shoulders, and then relax.

- **Visualization:** Take a moment and picture yourself in a calm and safe place. Visualize the details, such as colors, sounds, and smells, to create a sense of calm.

- **Mindfulness meditation:** Practice mindfulness by focusing on your breath and observing your thoughts without judgment. The purpose of this is to help you stay focused and reduce anxiety.

- **Affirmations:** Use positive affirmations to counteract negative thoughts and emotions. Repeat phrases like, "I am safe" or "I am in control of my emotions."

- **Aromatherapy:** Aromatherapy with calming scents like lavender or chamomile can help relax your mind and body.

 ## *Only Do What Feels Slightly Uncomfortable*

As you dive into your shadow work, it's important to challenge yourself, but not to the point of overwhelming discomfort. Aim to explore areas that are slightly uncomfortable, where you can grow without feeling entirely overwhelmed. This gradual approach allows for sustainable progress. A good rule of thumb is don't do more than 20% uncomfortable.

Safe Space Exercises

Begin by taking a deep breath and finding a comfortable position.

If you feel safe, gently close your eyes.

Be mindful of your breath.

Can you feel the rise and fall of your chest?

Observe the sensation as you inhale.

And notice how it feels as you exhale.

It's natural to be distracted by other thoughts or sounds that may come into your awareness.

That's perfectly okay.

Acknowledge these thoughts and sounds, and then let them drift away.

Return your attention to your breathing, recognizing how it ushers in calmness and stillness into your being.

Now, picture yourself in a unique place—a place where you experience safety, tranquility, and freedom.

This is a place brimming with serenity and delight.

Perhaps it's a location you've visited in the past, or maybe it's a place you're crafting with your imagination.

Take a moment to explore—what captures your attention?

What sights do you see, and what colors stand out?

What sounds surround you?

Is there a particular scent in the air?

Picture yourself in this sanctuary of yours.

What activities are you engaged in?

Feel the sense of calm and resilience washing over you as you recall your own strengths, skills, and unique qualities.

Before departing from your haven, take a final glance around and notice any other details that come into focus.

Remember, this is a special sanctuary that resides within you, a place you can revisit whenever you wish.

Each time you return, it serves as a reminder of your inner strength and the unique qualities that make you who you are.

Now, gently shift your attention back to your breath.

When you're ready, you may choose to open your eyes, carrying with you the feelings of tranquility and resilience.

Trigger Exercise

 ### Step 1: Recognize Your Emotional Triggers

The initial stage in effectively handling your emotional reactions is recognizing what triggers them. These triggers can encompass a wide range of things, including specific situations, events, or thoughts that evoke strong emotional responses within you. Examples of triggers may encompass scenarios like public speaking, criticism, financial challenges, or feelings of rejection.

To identify your personal triggers, take some time for self-reflection. Think back to your past experiences and recall situations or events that have ignited intense emotional reactions within you. Jot down instances that provoke strong emotions for you.

1. _____

_____

2. _____

_____

3. _____

_____

4. _____

_____

5. _____

_____

 ## Step 2: Describe Your Emotional Response

Once you've pinpointed your triggers, it's important to contemplate how you typically react when these triggers manifest in your life. This introspection can provide valuable insights into the impact these triggers have on your emotional well-being.

Reactions can vary widely and may encompass emotions such as anxiety, anger, or sadness. You might also notice physical reactions like trembling or perspiration. Honesty with yourself during this self-assessment is essential, as it will aid in identifying the most effective coping strategies for you. Write down your reactions.

1. _____

2. _____

3. _____

4. _____

5. _____

 ## Step 3: Cultivate Effective Coping Strategies

The final phase involves the development of coping strategies designed to manage your emotional responses when faced with triggers. Coping strategies can encompass a diverse array of techniques. As we discussed, this can include deep breathing exercises, mindfulness meditation, or practicing positive self-talk.

Selecting coping strategies that resonate with you and align with your comfort level is of paramount importance. Additionally, don't hesitate to experiment with various strategies to discover what works best for different situations. By cultivating these coping mechanisms, you empower yourself to regulate your emotional responses and diminish the impact that triggers have on your life.

In this chapter, we took a closer look at how to approach self-guided therapy and shadow work with safety and mindfulness. We explored various practical strategies and techniques to ensure that as you immerse yourself in the depths of your inner world, you do so with care and self-compassion.

Keep in mind that your path toward self-healing and personal growth is profound and filled with transformative moments. It's perfectly normal to have questions, concerns, and moments of apprehension as you move forward. We've equipped you with the tools to establish a secure and welcoming space for your personal development, including setting boundaries, recognizing your triggers, and crafting coping strategies.

In the forthcoming chapter, we will closely examine the beginning steps of shadow work. We'll uncover how to illuminate those concealed aspects of yourself and commence the journey of self-discovery. As you move ahead, have confidence in your ability to navigate the shadows and embrace the light that awaits you.

The exploration continues, and the potential for growth and self-understanding is boundless. So, turn the page with assurance, for the next chapter holds the key to unlocking your inner potential and uncovering the transformative essence of shadow work.

CHAPTER 4
SETTING FOOT ON THE
SHADOW PATH

Setting Foot on the Shadow Path

> *Our shadows hold the essence of who we are. They hold our most treasured gifts. By facing these aspects of ourselves, we become free to experience our glorious totality: the good and the bad, the dark and the light.* –**Debbie Ford**

My goal in this chapter is to provide you with simple yet effective strategies and methods to embark on your shadow work journey.

I want to emphasize that shadow work doesn't have to be overwhelming. In fact, we'll begin with simple, manageable steps designed with beginners like you in mind. My goal is to make this process as easy to understand and approach as possible. Remember, it's not about rushing through the work; it's about progressing at your own pace.

This is a space for optimism and growth, and I believe in your ability to make transformative changes in your life. You've already taken the first step by opening this workbook, and that's something to be proud of.

Are you ready to start on this journey of self-discovery and healing? Let's start by hearing Sebastian's story.

Sebastian had always been a man of grit and determination. His life's mission was to banish the word "wimp" from his vocabulary, a word that had haunted him since he was just five years old. It was a sunny afternoon when he and his father had taken a stroll in the park. Sebastian was a bundle of energy, but when he saw the pony ride, fear gripped his little heart. His father, a stern and imposing figure, looked down at him with a disapproving scowl.

"What kind of man are you going to make?" his father barked. "You're nothing but a little wimp, you're an embarrassment in our family."

Those words etched themselves into Sebastian's psyche, shaping the man he would become. From that day forward, he resolved to obliterate any trace of weakness within him.

As the years passed, Sebastian dedicated himself to the pursuit of strength and toughness, ignoring an entire part of his being. He became a black belt in karate, sculpted his body with weightlifting, and was always the first to volunteer for challenging tasks. He despised weakness, not only in himself but in others as well. He saw vulnerability as a character flaw, something to be eradicated at all costs.

Yet, despite all his efforts, he found himself haunted by moments when he felt like that little boy on the pony ride. There were times when he had to admit that he was still, in some areas of his life, a "wimp." It was in those moments that he had a strange revelation. Being a wimp had its advantages. It made him cautious, which kept him out of fights and, during his college years, prevented him from going out with friends when he knew heavy alcohol use was involved. This caution saved him from a tragic accident that claimed the life of his closest friend and severely injured others.

It was this life-altering event that prompted Sebastian to pause and reflect on the path he had been on. He had tried so hard to hide his weakness, to prove his worth to the world, that he had become someone he didn't even recognize. He chased dreams he didn't truly desire, filling his days with empty duties that left him feeling hollow.

One day, while watching a colleague struggle with a task at work, Sebastian muttered to himself, "He's such a wimp, and I hate wimps." But as the words escaped his lips, he felt a strange pang of self-awareness. He realized that his strong aversion to weakness in others was a reflection of his own neglect of his shadow self. It was a projection of his inner struggle to be perfect, to never show vulnerability or imperfection.

That moment of self-realization marked the beginning of Sebastian's journey into the depths of his own psyche. He decided to confront the shadows he had long buried within himself. He began to explore his own vulnerabilities, acknowledging that they were not signs of weakness but of his humanity.

Sebastian started to explore his shadow self. Through introspection and guided self-discovery, he unearthed buried emotions and confronted long-held beliefs about masculinity and strength. He learned that true strength didn't come from denying his vulnerabilities but from embracing them.

Over time, Sebastian transformed from a man obsessed with proving his toughness to one who understood the power of vulnerability and compassion. He repaired broken relationships and forged deeper connections with those around him. He no longer saw weakness in others as something to despise but as an opportunity for growth and understanding.

Sebastian's journey into his shadow self was not easy, but it was necessary for his personal growth and well-being. He discovered that accepting and integrating his "wimpish" tendencies allowed him to become a more authentic and empathetic person. In the end, he found that true strength was not in the absence of weakness but in the courage to confront and embrace it.

How to Spot Your Inner Shadow

In this part of your shadow work journey, we'll explore practical tips, exercises, and insights to help you identify and understand the hidden aspects of yourself that might be causing emotional turmoil. Remember, this is a safe and supportive space for you to grow and heal.

Triggers

Triggers are powerful messengers from your inner shadow, and they can be our best teachers if we pay attention to them. Here's a simple exercise to help you spot your triggers.

 ## *Exercise: Trigger Journal*

 Over the next week, whenever you feel emotionally charged—whether it's anger, frustration, sadness, or anxiety—write down the situation, the emotions you felt, and your immediate reactions.

Situation	Emotion	Reactions

After a week, review your entries. Write down any recurring themes, situations, or people that consistently trigger strong reactions in you. These patterns might indicate areas where your shadow is at work.

Repeating Unhealthy Patterns

Have you ever noticed that you keep making the same mistakes in your relationships or find yourself stuck in situations that seem to repeat like a broken record? These repetitive and often self-sabotaging patterns are often indicative of the influence of your shadow self.

Your shadow contains suppressed emotions, desires, and beliefs that you may not be consciously aware of. When these aspects of yourself remain unexamined and unacknowledged, they tend to manifest in your life as patterns that can be detrimental to your well-being.

Let's have a look at exactly how our shadow self can cause us to repeat unhealthy behavior patterns (Fosu, 2020):

◆ **Unconscious repression:** Your shadow self contains aspects of yourself that you have deemed unacceptable or have pushed away. These rejected parts can include unresolved traumas, fears, insecurities, and unmet needs. When these aspects are not integrated and addressed, they can drive you to repeat behaviors or make choices that lead to negative outcomes.

◆ **Seeking familiarity:** Human beings are creatures of habit, and we often seek out situations and relationships that feel familiar, even if they are unhealthy. Your shadow might be drawn to situations that replicate past experiences, whether they were positive or negative, as a way to maintain a sense of familiarity.

◆ **Projection onto others:** When your shadow remains unexplored, you may project these hidden aspects onto other people. For example, if you have unresolved anger within your shadow, you may consistently attract or clash with individuals who trigger that anger in you. This projection can perpetuate the cycle of unhealthy patterns.

 Exercise: Pattern Tracker

Think about recurring situations in your life where you've experienced negative outcomes or felt stuck. Write down these situations and the feelings associated with them.

Recurring Negative Situation	Feelings and Emotions

Now, identify the common threads among these situations. Jot down any similarities in how you react or the choices you make. These patterns may reveal your shadow's influence.

_____

_____

_____

_____

_____

Reflections

Have you ever noticed that you sometimes have strong negative reactions or judgments toward certain people? These reactions can be powerful clues to the existence of your inner shadow. When you dislike or judge someone intensely, it often indicates that they are triggering something within you. This is known as projection. We touched on this above briefly. Projection occurs when you unconsciously attribute qualities, emotions, or behaviors that you don't want to acknowledge in yourself to someone else (Projection, 2022).

 Mirror Exercise

 Write down a list of people you strongly dislike or have conflicts with. Then, for each person, write down the qualities or behaviors that bother you about them.

Names	Qualities that Bother You

I would like you to take a moment to review this list. Write down any of these qualities that resonate with something you dislike or deny about yourself. This can be a powerful way to uncover hidden aspects of your shadow.

Dreams

Dreams are windows into the subconscious, and they often reveal our shadow selves. Dreams have long been regarded as a powerful tool for exploring the subconscious mind, and they play a crucial role in the process of shadow work. Your dreams are a canvas upon which your unconscious mind paints its stories, thoughts, emotions, and symbols. While your conscious mind is at rest, your unconscious self becomes more accessible, allowing hidden aspects of your psyche, including your shadow, to emerge.

Did you know that dreams often communicate in symbols and metaphors, making them a unique language of the unconscious? These symbols can represent repressed emotions, unresolved conflicts, and aspects of your shadow self that you may not be fully aware of in your waking life.

 ## *Exercise: Dream Journal*

 Keep this page open and by your bedside, along with a pen. Upon waking from a dream, immediately jot down everything you remember, including the storyline, characters, emotions, and any prominent symbols or events. Don't worry about making sense of it just yet; capture the raw details.

Dream 1:

_____

_____

_____

_____

Dream 2:

_____

_____

_____

_____

_____

_____

Dream 3:

_____

_____

_____

_____

_____

Dream 4:

_____

_____

_____

_____

_____

Over time, review your dream journal and write down any recurring themes, symbols, or emotions. Pay special attention to dreams that evoke strong emotional reactions, whether positive or negative.

_____

_____

_____

_____

_____

 Ask yourself if there are any aspects of your shadow self that seem to be emerging through your dreams. Write down any patterns or conflicts that parallel your waking experiences.

_____

_____

_____

_____

_____

_____

Fears and Reactions

Your fears and reactions are like signs on the road of self-discovery, pointing toward the hidden aspects of your shadow self. Your fears often conceal valuable information about your shadow self. These fears may be linked to experiences, traumas, or aspects of your personality that you've suppressed or denied. They can include fears of rejection, abandonment, failure, vulnerability, or even success.

 ## *Exercise: Fear Exploration*

 Write down a list of your strongest fears or anxieties.

1. _____

_____

2. _____

_____

3. _____

_____

4. _____

_____

5. _____

_____

For each fear, write down how you typically react when confronted by it.

Fear	Reaction

 Jot down whether you feel these reactions are appropriate or rooted in past experiences.

_____

_____

_____

_____

_____

_____

By trying out these practical exercises, you'll gain valuable insights into your inner shadow. Remember to do them at your own pace and always take breaks when you feel overwhelmed.

Did you know that research tells us that confronting our shadow selves can offer us increased emotional intelligence, better mental health, and improved relationships (Guil et al., 2021)?

Maxine's Story

Meet Maxine, a woman who had been grappling with anxiety and emotional turmoil for as long as she could remember. At her workplace, she often found herself entangled in conflicts with her colleagues, and her stress levels were through the roof. She couldn't understand why she felt so out of control when it came to her emotions and her interactions with others.

One day, feeling at her wit's end, Maxine decided to give shadow work a try. She had heard about the power of it and was eager to explore her inner world to find answers to her struggles.

As Maxine looked more closely into her shadow work, she began to unravel the layers of her past. She realized that many of her triggers at work were connected to her childhood experiences of feeling powerless and unheard. Growing up, Maxine had often felt overshadowed by her siblings, leading her to believe that her voice didn't matter.

Through introspection and journaling, Maxine uncovered that she had been projecting her own deep-seated insecurities onto her colleagues. Her tendency to interpret innocent comments as personal attacks was a defense mechanism she had developed to protect herself from feeling powerless once more. She recognized that her emotional reactions were not solely about her coworkers but were rooted in her unresolved past.

Acknowledging her projections and the source of her emotional turmoil was a pivotal moment for Maxine. It wasn't an easy realization to confront, but it was the first step toward healing and personal growth. It was at this time that Maxine began to address her insecurities and childhood wounds.

She learned healthier coping mechanisms for dealing with her anxiety and triggers. Mindfulness and breathing exercises helped her stay grounded in the present moment, preventing her from spiraling into emotional chaos. Maxine also worked on developing better communication skills, allowing her to express herself without feeling threatened.

As Maxine continued her shadow work journey, a transformation took place within her. She started to notice significant improvements in her relationships at work. Instead of reacting defensively, she responded with empathy and understanding. Her colleagues began to perceive her as approachable and open, leading to more harmonious interactions.

Maxine's inner peace grew as she integrated the repressed aspects of her shadow. She no longer felt controlled by her emotions, and the weight of her childhood insecurities began to lift. Her newfound self-awareness allowed her to regulate her emotions more effectively, and she felt a sense of empowerment she had never experienced before.

Maxine's story serves as a powerful example of how shadow work can lead to self-awareness, personal growth, and emotional regulation. By acknowledging and addressing the hidden aspects of her shadow, she not only improved her relationships but also found inner peace and a deeper sense of self.

Unpacking Your Core and Shadow Beliefs

Let's look a little closer at core and shadow beliefs. These are the foundational beliefs that shape how you perceive yourself, others, and the world around you. Identifying and transmuting these beliefs is a powerful way to regain control over your emotions, heal, and experience positive transformation.

Here are some common core beliefs that do not help us:

◆ **I am not enough:** Many of us carry the belief that we are not worthy of love, success, or happiness. This belief can lead to feelings of inadequacy and self-doubt.

◆ **I am unlovable:** This belief can stem from past experiences of rejection or abandonment, leading to feelings of isolation and loneliness.

◆ **I must be perfect:** Striving for perfection can be paralyzing, causing anxiety and fear of failure.

◆ **I am a victim:** Believing that you are always at the mercy of external circumstances can disempower you and lead to resentment and anger.

◆ **I am responsible for everyone's happiness:** This belief can lead to people pleasing and neglecting your own needs, resulting in exhaustion and frustration.

We need to ask ourselves how we can change our perspective on these:

◆ **Self-awareness:** The first step is to become aware of your core beliefs. Pay attention to recurring thoughts and emotions. Journaling can be a helpful tool for this. Write down moments when you feel unworthy, unlovable, or overwhelmed.

◆ **Question your beliefs:** Challenge these beliefs. Ask yourself, "Is this belief based on facts or past experiences? Is it serving me well?" Often, you'll find that these beliefs are based on outdated information or other people's opinions.

◆ **Replace with empowering beliefs:** Once you've identified a disempowering belief, consciously choose to replace it with a more positive and empowering one. For example, replace "I am not enough" with "I am worthy of love and success just as I am."

◆ **Affirmations:** Create affirmations that support your new beliefs. Repeat them daily to reinforce the positive change. Affirmations can be a powerful tool for reprogramming your mind.

Cognitive Distortions

These are thought patterns that often lead to negative emotions and behaviors. They can be like a fog that clouds our judgment, making it challenging to see the truth about ourselves and the world around us. In shadow work, recognizing these distortions is crucial because they often connect to the hidden aspects of our psyche.

Here are some examples of cognitive distortions (Grinspoon, 2022):

◆ **Personalization:** Blaming oneself for events that are beyond their control. Example: "Our team lost because of me."

◆ **Catastrophizing:** Magnifying problems and imagining the worst-case scenarios. Example: "This spot on my skin is probably skin cancer; I'll be dead soon."

◆ **Fortune-telling:** Predicting negative outcomes without concrete evidence. Example: "My cholesterol is going to be sky-high."

- **Emotional reasoning:** Letting emotions dictate beliefs rather than relying on facts. Example: "I feel worthless, so I must be worthless."

- **Jumping to conclusions (mind-reading):** Assuming others' thoughts and intentions without evidence. Example: "The doctor is going to tell me I have cancer."

- **Black-and-white (all-or-nothing) thinking:** Seeing things as either perfect or a complete failure. Example: "I never have anything interesting to say."

- **Should-ing and must-ing:** Using self-critical language that imposes unnecessary pressure. Example: "I should be losing weight."

- **Overgeneralization:** Drawing broad, negative conclusions from a single event. Example: "I had one unhealthy meal; I'll always be unhealthy."

- **Comparison:** Measuring oneself against others without complete knowledge. Example: "All of my coworkers are happier than me."

- **Mental filter:** Focusing solely on negative aspects, ignoring positive elements. Example: "I am terrible at getting enough sleep."

- **Magnification and minimization:** Exaggerating negatives while downplaying positives. Example: "It was just one healthy meal."

- **Labeling:** Assigning negative labels to oneself based on past mistakes. Example: "I'm just not a healthy person."

- **Disqualifying the positive:** Dismissing positive achievements as luck or insignificant. Example: "I answered that well, but it was a lucky guess."

Exercise: Identifying Cognitive Distortions

 Take a moment to reflect on your thoughts and emotions throughout the day. When you find yourself experiencing a negative feeling, try to pinpoint the thought that triggered it. Ask yourself the following question:

What thought preceded this emotion? For example, if you're feeling anxious, the thought might be, "I'll never be good enough."

Negative Feeling	Thought Proceeding Negative Feeling

Write down which cognitive distortion this thought falls into. Use the list you've been provided above to identify the specific distortion(s). For instance, if the thought is all-or-nothing thinking (e.g., "I'll never be good enough"), write that down.

Thought	Cognitive Distortion

Being mindful of cognitive distortions is a huge step toward uncovering your shadow beliefs and experiencing personal growth. Take your time, be gentle with yourself, and remember that it's normal to encounter these distortions—what matters is how you address them.

Analyzing Your Triggers

Triggers are situations, events, or even words that bring up strong and often uncomfortable emotions within us. They can make us feel out of control, and it's crucial to recognize them so you can work through them effectively.

You might be wondering how you can identify a trigger. You should start by paying close attention to your emotional reactions. Here's how:

- **Notice unusual emotional intensity:** If you find yourself feeling extremely angry, anxious, sad, or any intense emotion that seems out of proportion to the situation, that's a clue.

- **Take a step back:** When you notice such intense emotions, pause for a moment. Ask yourself if what just happened warrants this level of reaction. Is the situation really as bad as it seems at that moment?

Remember, triggers are your subconscious mind's way of alerting you to unresolved issues. Here's what you can do next:

- **Pause and breathe:** When you notice a trigger, the first step is to pause. Take a deep breath. This simple act can help you regain control over your emotions.

- **Self-compassion:** Be gentle with yourself. It's okay to feel what you feel. Your emotions are valid, even if they seem disproportionate. Try saying to yourself, "It's okay, I'm just triggered right now, and that's okay."

- **Ask, "Why?":** Reflect on why this situation triggered such a strong reaction. Dig deep into your past experiences and beliefs. Often, triggers are connected to unresolved issues from your past.

Studies have shown that recognizing and working through triggers is a vital part of emotional regulation and personal growth. By addressing these triggers, individuals can experience reduced anxiety, improved emotional stability, and enhanced overall well-being (Veazey, 2022). So, rest assured, you're on the right path.

Interactive Element

 ### *Exercise: Examine Your Inner "Tapes"*

 Take some time to think about the negative comments or criticisms that others have made about you. It could be something a parent, friend, or even a colleague said. Write them down.

_____

_____

_____

_____

_____

_____

_____

Reflect on the beliefs you hold about yourself that are negative or self-critical. Write them down.

Recall moments in your life when these negative beliefs about yourself did not hold true. List examples of when you proved these beliefs wrong.

Identify evidence that contradicts these negative beliefs. What strengths, achievements, or qualities do you possess that show you are not defined by these beliefs?

_____

_____

_____

_____

_____

_____

_____

_____

Exercise: Unpack Your Triggers

> Recall a recent situation where you felt an intense emotional reaction. Write down the triggering event in detail.

_____

_____

_____

_____

_____

_____

_____

> Consider not only the physical manifestation (e.g., yelling, crying) but, more importantly, the feelings driving that physical manifestation. Write down your emotional response.

_____

_____

_____

_____

_____

Write down why you think you reacted the way you did. Were there underlying emotions or past experiences that contributed to your reaction?

_____

_____

_____

_____

_____

Core Beliefs Journal Prompts

Use these prompts to journal and explore your core beliefs.

If I could change anything about myself it would be...

_____

_____

_____

_____

_____

_____

I feel most vulnerable when...

I learned this belief from...

I can challenge this belief by...

_____

_____

_____

_____

_____

_____

I believe I am worthy of love and acceptance because...

_____

_____

_____

_____

_____

_____

In this chapter, I've laid the foundation for your journey by providing practical and easy-to-understand steps for self-reflection and understanding your triggers. You've begun to shine a light on those hidden corners of your psyche, where your shadow self resides.

Shadow work is a gentle, compassionate journey of self-discovery and healing. You've already shown great courage by embarking on this adventure, and for that, you should be proud.

In the chapters to come, we'll dive even deeper, customizing a toolbox of specialized techniques for shadow work. These techniques will help you navigate the complexities of your inner world and guide you toward greater self-awareness, emotional regulation, and personal growth.

So, take a moment to acknowledge your bravery, your desire for self-healing, and your commitment to growth. The road ahead may have its challenges, but it's also filled with incredible rewards.

Turn the page, and let's delve deeper into your shadow work toolbox. The adventure continues!

Illuminate The Path For Those Who Walk Behind You on This Journey of Self-Discovery

In the labyrinth of self-discovery, where the corridors of our subconscious hide the keys to our most profound insights, a powerful tool lies: self-guided shadow work. For those who have embarked on this introspective journey, you know the transformative power these pages hold. They are not mere collections of paper but vessels of self-revelation, guiding us through the murky waters of our inner world.

Now, imagine standing at the edge of a vast ocean, the waves whispering secrets of ancient wisdom. This ocean is the collective consciousness of all who seek understanding, healing, and growth through shadow work. This workbook and journal are not just your boat in this vastness but also your map and compass. The insights you've gleaned, the revelations unearthed, and the transformations undergone are treasures you've discovered along the way.

However, a treasure shared is a treasure multiplied. Leaving a review for this workbook and journal casts a stone into this vast ocean, creating ripples that extend far beyond your sight. Each ripple reaches others navigating their own introspective journeys, guiding them, encouraging them, and letting them know they are not alone in these uncharted waters.

Your review serves as a lighthouse for fellow travelers lost in the fog of their subconscious. It offers hope and reassurance that their path, though challenging, is traversable and transformative. Your words can illuminate the benefits of shadow work, shedding light on how it has changed your perspective, relationships, and life.

Sharing your challenges and triumphs can inspire others to take the first step, pick up this workbook, and confront their shadows with hope and determination.

Thank you for your bravery, your vulnerability, and your support. Your voice matters, and your experience is a gift to those who seek to follow in your footsteps. Together, we can help others find the courage to face their shadows and emerge into the light of profound self-awareness and healing.

Scan the QR code to leave your review!

CHAPTER 5
THE TOOLBOX-
SPECIALIZED
TECHNIQUES FOR
SHADOW WORK

The Toolbox-Specialized Techniques for Shadow Work

> *Unless you learn to face your own shadows, you will continue to see them in others, because the world outside of you is only a reflection of the world inside of you.* **–The Minds Journal**

We're taking another step forward, and I'm excited to share a toolbox filled with more shadow work techniques. These techniques can be added to the ones explored in the previous chapter to build the strategies you need to continue.

In this chapter, I've included the techniques with you in mind. They are simple, budget-friendly, and tailored to beginners like yourself. As usual, the goal is to create a safe and inviting space where you can explore your shadow self at your own pace without feeling overwhelmed.

Each one is a tool that can help you uncover hidden aspects of yourself, understand your emotions, and, ultimately, transform your life for the better.

Let's begin.

The Dialogue Exercise: Talking to Your Shadow

Find a quiet and comfortable space where you won't be disturbed. Sit or lie down in a relaxed position, and take a few deep breaths to center yourself.

Close your eyes and imagine yourself in front of a group of hypercritical people, or even just one person, who tends to trigger feelings of insecurity and self-consciousness within you. It could be someone from your past or present.

 **Now, see yourself through their eyes. Write down what you think you look like to them. This version of yourself, the one you see from their perspective, is your shadow. It might look very different from the person you typically think of as "you."**

_____

_____

_____

_____

_____

_____

_____

_____

Focus on this version of yourself, your Shadow, without judgment. Acknowledge its presence and understand that it's a part of you, just like any other aspect.

In your mind, reach out and form an unbreakable bond with your Shadow. Imagine a strong connection between you and it. Feel this connection physically, as if you are holding hands, hugging, or simply being close to it.

Speak to your Shadow with kindness and assurance. Say, "You're with me at all times." As you say these words, imagine the bond growing stronger, and feel the connection becoming more tangible.

Recognize that by forming this bond, you are taking the first step toward a powerful tool known as "Inner Authority." It's an authority that emanates from within yourself, allowing you and your Shadow to speak with one unified voice.

Embrace this newfound authority. It's different from what you're accustomed to because it arises from deep within you, integrating all aspects of your being.

With your Inner Authority, you can begin to explore and heal in ways you might not have thought possible. Your shadow is no longer something to be feared or ignored but a valuable part of your journey towards self-discovery and growth.

Take a moment to sit in this newfound awareness, appreciating the connection you've formed with your Shadow and the Inner Authority that is now at your disposal.

The Visualization Exercise: A Mental Journey

This meditation is designed to create a safe and introspective space where you can explore and integrate your shadow aspects.

 Begin by setting a clear intention for your meditation. Write down what you hope to gain from this experience and what you are ready to release. Is there a specific emotion, fear, or negative behavior you'd like to explore and understand better? Take a moment to clarify your intentions.

_____

_____

_____

_____

_____

_____

_____

_____

Find a calm, quiet spot where you won't be bothered. It could be in your cozy room or a peaceful outdoor area where you feel relaxed.

◆ Choose a position you feel comfortable and safe in. Take some slow, deep breaths to relax your body and let go of any tension in your muscles. Try to block out any distractions and focus your attention inside yourself.

◆ Concentrate on your breathing. As you breathe in and out, let your breath be like an anchor that calms your thoughts. You should expect your mind to wander this is normal. Gently take a breath and bring it back to the present.

◆ Start imagining your shadow self. Picture any hidden emotions, fears, or negative habits that you usually keep buried. Don't judge or push them away just let them come into your mind.

◆ Accept your shadow self with an open heart. Realize that these parts of you are just as natural as any other and not necessarily good or bad. Let go of any preconceived ideas and simply acknowledge that they are a part of you.

◆ Now, I want you to visualize yourself physically letting go of the emotional baggage you've been holding onto. Picture your fears, insecurities, and negative habits as heavy burdens. With each breath out, imagine these burdens getting lighter, leaving you feeling freer.

◆ Slowly merge your shadow self with your conscious awareness. Understand that by doing this, you're becoming more complete and genuine. Imagine your light and shadow aspects coming together, creating a balanced and harmonious inner self.

As you finish this visualization, take a moment to write down any new thoughts or feelings that came up during the process. Remember, shadow work is an ongoing journey; each time you explore it, you'll discover more about yourself and grow.

A Role-Playing Exercise: Embodying Your Shadow

Find a quiet and comfortable space where you won't be disturbed. Take a few deep breaths to relax and center yourself.

 Write down aspects of yourself or emotions that you may have been suppressing, denying, or avoiding. These are often elements of your shadow self.

1. _____

   _____

2. _____

   _____

3. _____

   _____

4. _____

   _____

5. _____

   _____

6. _____

   _____

Now, write down one specific aspect or emotion you want to explore during this exercise. It could be anger, jealousy, fear, insecurity, or any other emotion or trait.

 Write down a name and a persona to the aspect of your shadow self you've chosen. Imagine this character as a separate entity, distinct from your usual self.

Character Name:

_____

Character Persona:

_____

_____

_____

_____

_____

_____

Write down a description of the character's appearance, personality, and behaviors. How does this persona express the chosen shadow aspect?

Character's Appearance:

_____

_____

_____

_____

_____

_____

Character's Personality:

_____

_____

_____

_____

_____

_____

Character's Behaviors:

_____

_____

_____

_____

_____

_____

Character's Emotions:

_____

_____

_____

_____

_____

_____

Begin to embody your created persona. Act out or role-play as this character. Imagine how they would react in different situations. Pay attention to how it feels to express the chosen shadow aspect through this character. Write down any physical sensations, emotions, or thoughts that arise.

Physical Sensations:

Emotions:

Thoughts:

After a few minutes of role-playing, pause and return to your normal self. Write down your experiences and observations. Answer questions like:

What did it feel like to express this shadow aspect through the persona?

_____

_____

_____

_____

_____

_____

_____

Were there any surprising insights or emotions that emerged during the role-playing?

_____

_____

_____

_____

_____

_____

How did your body react to this exploration?

Did you notice any resistance or discomfort?

What did you learn about this aspect of your shadow self?

_____

_____

_____

_____

_____

_____

_____

Reflect on how you can integrate the insights gained from this exercise into your daily life. Consider whether there are healthy ways to express and address this shadow aspect.

You can repeat this exercise with different aspects of your shadow self over time to gain a deeper understanding of your inner dynamics.

The Affirmation Exercise: Reinforcing Positive Change

Reflect on the affirmations, one by one. Take a few deep breaths and repeat the affirmation to yourself several times. Allow each affirmation to sink in and resonate with you.

 After repeating the affirmation, write your thoughts and feelings about it. Explore any emotions that come up and consider how the affirmation relates to your life, experiences, and inner self.

Affirmations	Thoughts & Feelings Evoked
1. I choose to face my issues.	
2. I am not to blame for my trauma.	
3. I deserve respect.	
4. I will live in the present.	
5. I am going to grow and learn from pain.	
6. I am in love with who I am.	
7. I forgive myself for my shadow side.	
8. I am grateful.	

9. I acknowledge and accept my true self.	
10. My mistakes do not define me.	
11. My past is not my future.	
12. I am worthy of love.	
13. I am learning who I am as a whole.	
14. I can decide my future.	
15. I want to move forward.	
16. I want to heal.	
17. I will no longer hold grudges.	
18. I own my mistakes.	
19. I only need validation from me.	
20. Those who are mean do not deserve my energy.	
21. I deserve boundaries.	
22. Owning my emotions makes me stronger.	
23. The person I'm becoming is amazing.	
24. I choose to learn from my mistakes.	

For each affirmation, think about how you can incorporate it into your daily life and shadow work journey. What actions or mindset shifts can you make to align with the affirmation?

Continue this process with each selected affirmation, taking your time to truly internalize and work with each one.

 Finally, consider how these affirmations collectively contribute to your shadow work and personal development. Write down the progress you've made and the areas where you still have room for growth.

_____

_____

_____

_____

_____

_____

_____

Repeat this exercise regularly to deepen your shadow work and self-awareness. Over time, you may find that these affirmations help you uncover and heal hidden aspects of yourself while empowering you to move forward with a more positive and self-compassionate mindset.

The Self-Compassion Exercise: Embracing Your Shadow with Love

Sit or lie down in a comfortable position. You can also do this exercise while standing or walking if that feels more natural to you.

To start, take a few deep cleansing breaths. In through your nose and out through your mouth. Continue to breathe deeply and slowly, paying full attention to your breath.

Close your eyes and bring to mind an aspect of yourself or a past event you have been avoiding or denying, representing your shadow self. It could be a negative belief, a past mistake, or a quality you're not proud of.

While focusing on this aspect of your shadow, repeat self-compassionate phrases silently in your mind, such as:

- ✅ "I acknowledge and accept this part of myself."

- ✅ "I am human, and I make mistakes."

- ✅ "It's okay to have flaws and imperfections."

- ✅ "I am worthy of love and acceptance, even with this shadow."

As you continue to breathe and repeat these phrases, visualize a warm and loving light surrounding the aspect of yourself or the event that represents your shadow. Imagine this light enveloping it with acceptance and understanding.

As you continue to breathe and visualize, imagine that this aspect of your shadow is starting to soften and dissolve. Feel any tension or resistance in your body slowly releasing.

Offer yourself kindness and forgiveness for carrying this shadow. Remind yourself that you are not defined by your shadow, and it is a part of your humanity.

With your eyes still closed, place your hand on your heart as a physical gesture of self-compassion. Feel the warmth and connection to your own heart.

Conclude the meditation by expressing gratitude to yourself for engaging in this self-compassion exercise and for your willingness to work with your shadow.

When you're ready, slowly open your eyes and return to the present moment.

 This self-compassion meditation can help you integrate and make peace with your shadow self. It allows you to connect with your inner self and provide the love and acceptance that every part of you deserves. Feel free to write down any emotions you felt during your meditation.

The Art Therapy Exercise: Expressing Your Shadow Creatively

Before beginning this exercise, you will want to gather the following materials:

- ✓ Blank canvas or paper

- ✓ Various art supplies—colored pencils, markers, acrylic paints, charcoal, pastels.

- ✓ Brushes if you're using paint.

- ✓ Water and a container for your brushes.

- ✓ An open and curious mindset.

Create a calm and inviting environment for your art therapy session. Play soothing music, light a candle, or do whatever helps you get into a creative and introspective mood.

 Take a few moments to reflect on the aspects of yourself or past experiences that you consider to be part of your shadow self. These could be qualities, emotions, or memories that you've suppressed, denied, or are reluctant to acknowledge. Take a moment to write them down.

_____

_____

_____

_____

_____

_____

_____

_____

_____

_____

_____

◆ Select an art medium that resonates with you and feels comfortable. You can choose to work with colors, paint, charcoal, or any other medium that allows you to express yourself.

◆ Begin by creating a self-portrait on your canvas or paper. It doesn't need to be highly detailed or realistic; the focus here is on self-expression. Capture your facial expression, posture, and any emotions you associate with your shadow self.

◆ Use colors, shapes, and symbols to represent the aspects of your shadow self within the self-portrait. For example, if you're exploring feelings of anger or sadness, you might use red or blue hues to convey those emotions. If you're exploring a particular quality, like perfectionism, you could incorporate patterns or symbols that represent that trait.

◆ Allow yourself to express your feelings and thoughts through your art freely. Don't worry about making it look "good" or "perfect." This is about honest expression.

◆ As you work on your self-portrait, engage in an internal dialogue with the aspects of your shadow self. Ask questions like, "Why are you here?" "What do you need?" "How can I integrate or understand you better?" Write down any insights or responses that come up during this process.

 Take breaks to step back and contemplate your artwork. What do the colors, shapes, and symbols tell you about your shadow self? What emotions are emerging as you work on this piece? Write down your answers below.

_____

_____

_____

_____

_____

_____

_____

Once your self-portrait feels complete, sit with it for a while. Reflect on what you've created and the insights you've gained through the process.

Remember that art therapy is a deeply personal and therapeutic process. There are no right or wrong ways to create your self-portrait, and it's more about the process of self-discovery and expression than the final result. Be gentle with yourself and use this exercise as an opportunity to explore and understand your shadow self in a creative and healing way.

Interactive Element: Deep Shadow Work Journal Prompts

Journaling is a valuable tool in the world of shadow work. If you struggle with what to write, you should know this is normal, and it happens to all of us. I wanted to include a lot of journal prompts to help you with that.

What values were instilled in you during your upbringing?

_____

_____

_____

_____

Identify the triggers that cause physical tension in your body.

_____

_____

_____

How would your friends and family describe your personality?

_____

_____

_____

_____

What aspects of yourself do you wish your friends and family were aware of?

_____

_____

_____

_____

Share something you find challenging to confess to others.

_____

_____

_____

_____

What skills or abilities do you wish you could improve upon?

_____

_____

_____

_____

Reflect on the three most significant relationships in your life and how they have shaped your self-perception.

_____

_____

_____

_____

What types of individuals are drawn to you as friends or acquaintances?

_____

_____

_____

_____

Anonymously share a personal secret with the world if given the chance.

_____

_____

_____

_____

Describe the time and circumstances when you last experienced genuine inner peace.

_____

_____

_____

_____

What aspects of yourself make you feel inferior to others, and how do colleagues at work perceive you?

_____

_____

_____

_____

What misconceptions do people commonly hold about you in your professional life?

_____

_____

_____

_____

What do you wish people at work understood better about you?

_____

_____

_____

_____

If you could start your career anew, what choices or actions would you change?

_____

_____

_____

_____

What work-related responsibilities drain your energy the most?

_____

_____

_____

_____

Explore the work requests that evoke negative reactions within you and examine the reasons behind them.

_____

_____

_____

_____

What changes would you make in your workplace or career if you could?

_____

_____

_____

_____

Do you desire a different manner of treatment from your colleagues at work? If so, how?

_____

_____

_____

_____

Identify the expectations at work that feel challenging to meet.

_____

_____

_____

As we conclude this chapter, you've taken the necessary steps in constructing your personal toolbox for shadow work—a collection of introspective and self-awareness tools that will serve as your companions on this transformative journey. You've delved into various prompts and techniques, gaining insights into your hidden aspects, inner conflicts, and unresolved emotions. Remember, shadow work is an ongoing process, and your toolbox will continue to evolve and grow.

In the next chapter, we will explore even more powerful and practical strategies to deepen your understanding of yourself, confront buried traumas, and navigate the complexities of your inner world. These advanced but still easy-to-understand tools will equip you with the means to unravel deeper layers of your psyche, fostering growth, healing, and self-acceptance. Prepare to explore the uncharted territories of your consciousness, armed with a wealth of knowledge and newfound resilience.

CHAPTER 6

FURTHER INTO THE

SHADOWS

Further Into the Shadows

>  *What you are, you do not see. What you see is your shadow. –*
> ***Rabindranath Tagore***

In the previous chapters, we've laid the foundation, explored the basics, and even started working with some practical skills to help you navigate the uncharted territories of your inner world. You are doing an incredible job!

Now, it's time to take a slightly deeper plunge into the waters of shadow work. But don't worry we won't be diving into anything too overwhelming or intimidating. This chapter is designed to gently introduce you to more advanced shadow work concepts and techniques without pushing you too far.

If you're feeling a bit apprehensive about this next step, that's perfectly normal. Remember, shadow work is a journey, and taking it at your own pace is entirely okay. We're here to support you every step of the way, providing guidance, compassion, and understanding.

As we venture into more advanced concepts, remember that this is all in service of your personal growth and self-healing. The goal isn't perfection; it's progress. So, take a deep breath, trust the process, and know you're in good hands.

In the following pages, I'll offer you techniques that will empower you to navigate the complexities of your inner world with greater ease and understanding. You'll uncover ways to heal old wounds, release what no longer serves you, and further integrate the various facets of your whole self.

I believe in your capacity for growth and healing.

Unveiling Your Childhood

Let's begin by shining a light on your childhood and those wounds that might still be affecting you today. We all carry baggage from our past, and recognizing these wounds is the first step in healing. Here are some common examples (Sansone et al., 2012):

♦ **Abandonment:** This wound can stem from a caregiver's absence or inconsistency in your early years. It might manifest as an intense fear of rejection or a tendency to cling to relationships for fear of being left alone.

♦ **Neglect:** Childhood neglect, whether emotional or physical, can lead to feelings of unworthiness or self-doubt. You might find it hard to prioritize your needs or have a constant inner critic.

♦ **Trauma:** Traumatic experiences during childhood can leave deep scars. These could include physical, emotional, or sexual abuse. The signs may be vivid nightmares, flashbacks, or severe anxiety.

♦ **Criticism:** Constant criticism from parents or authority figures can lead to low self-esteem and a harsh inner critic. You might struggle with perfectionism and a constant need for external validation.

♦ **Loss:** Losing a loved one at a young age can create issues around grief and loss that linger into adulthood. It might manifest as difficulties in forming and maintaining relationships.

Knowing how to recognize that your inner child is wounded is key. If you want to explore inner child healing and any hurts or traumas from childhood, I would like to recommend the last book I published, Reparent Your Wounded Inner Child. It is a gentle, helpful tool to take on that journey with you. Now, let's review some signs that may resonate with your inner wounded child:

- **Emotional overreactions:** You find yourself reacting strongly to situations that may seem minor to others.

- **Repetition of patterns:** You notice that you keep repeating the same destructive patterns in relationships or life choices.

- **Self-sabotage:** You engage in self-destructive behaviors, perhaps unconsciously, like procrastination, substance abuse, or self-harm.

- **Low self-esteem:** You struggle with self-worth, often feeling like you're not good enough.

- **Avoidance:** You avoid confronting your past, either by numbing your emotions or diverting your attention.

Our childhood experiences shape our beliefs and behaviors. During your formative years, you learned how to navigate the world around you, but sometimes, you picked up limiting beliefs and coping mechanisms that no longer serve you.

For instance, if you grew up in an environment where emotions were repressed, you might have learned to suppress your own feelings. If you faced constant criticism, you might have developed perfectionistic tendencies. These learned behaviors and beliefs can influence your adult life in ways you might not even be aware of.

Jesse's Story

Growing up with a mentally ill mother impacted me far beyond my ability to comprehend until recently. I carried my work stress home. If I was working on a project, any project, it had to be perfect, even if that meant staying late or working on it at home well into the night. I never looked into a mirror and felt confident. I would starve myself, even as an adult, if I got dressed in the morning and anything felt tight. My appearance needed to be perfect, or I wouldn't be accepted. In any relationship I had, I would spiral at the slightest comment. It could be something as simple as "Hey, could we meet an hour later tomorrow? Something has come up." I would hear: *They want to limit how much time we spend together because I am so annoying.*

You see, I grew up with a father who criticized everything I ever did. I was never smart enough. I was never funny enough. I was never fit enough. As an adult, this formed my need for perfectionism. This was my coping mechanism. What I found out through shadow work was I never believed any of these things about myself. In fact, I found myself to be pretty awesome. These were the beliefs of my father, not me. I was able to relax, let go of needing to be perfect all the time, and uncover my true self.

Healing Exercises

Now, let's talk about the good stuff–healing. Remember, this is a process, and it's okay to take it one step at a time. Here are some practical strategies to help you begin your healing journey:

 Start by offering yourself the same compassion you'd give to anyone you love. Jot down five things you truly admire about yourself.

1. _____

_____

2. _____

_____

3. _____

_____

4. _____

_____

5. _____

_____

Write down your thoughts, feelings, and memories of your childhood. What do you think you may still be holding on to? This can help you gain insight into your past and how it's affecting your present.

_____

_____

_____

_____

_____

Consider talking to someone you trust, like a good friend. They can provide guidance and a safe space for exploring your childhood wounds and have a perspective you may not be able to see just yet. Write down anything you learned from your conversation.

_____

_____

_____

_____

_____

_____

Visualize and connect with your inner child. Write down five things you want to say to them. Remind them you are there to love and support them now. This can be a powerful way to heal past wounds.

1. _____

2. _____

3. _____

4. _____

5. _____

Learning to set healthy boundaries is vital for protecting yourself from repeating old patterns of hurt. Write down three boundaries you want to put in place and one you are going to put in place immediately.

1. _____

2. _____

3. _____

◆ **Circle the boundary you will put in place immediatly.**

This is the time to be gentle with yourself and celebrate every small step forward. Studies have shown that childhood wounds can have a significant impact on our mental and emotional well-being throughout our lives. Research indicates that addressing these wounds through self-reflection can lead to improved mental health, healthier relationships, and increased overall life satisfaction (Sansone et al., 2012).

Using Your Guilt as a Tool

Let's start by demystifying guilt. Guilt is that uncomfortable feeling we experience when we believe we've done something wrong or failed to meet our own or society's standards. It's a common emotion that can be triggered by various situations or actions. While it may initially seem like a burden, guilt serves a valuable purpose in our lives.

Think of guilt as a mirror reflecting your values and moral compass. It's your conscience nudging you to pay attention to something important. When you feel guilty, it's often a sign that there's something within you that needs your attention and understanding.

Guilt can be closely tied to your shadow self. Your shadow self is the part of you that contains unacknowledged or suppressed emotions, desires, and experiences. Guilt can often be a manifestation of these hidden aspects, trying to get your attention.

Embracing guilt means embracing an opportunity for growth. When you confront your guilt head-on, you're taking a brave step toward understanding yourself better. It's a chance to bring those shadowy aspects into the light and work through them.

Managing Unhelpful Guilt Exercises

Now that you understand the purpose of guilt let's explore some exercises to manage it effectively. Remember, our goal is not to eliminate guilt but to harness its power for your personal development.

Self-Compassion

Begin by showing yourself kindness and understanding. Understand that it's okay to feel guilty sometimes; it's a part of being human. Treat yourself as you would a close friend, with love and empathy.

 Write down a recent guilt-inducing situation. Then, list three ways to offer yourself self-compassion in response to this guilt.

1. _____

_____

2. _____

_____

3. _____

_____

Identify the Root Cause

Explore the underlying cause of your guilt. Ask yourself why you feel this way and what values or beliefs are being challenged. This can help you unearth hidden aspects of your shadow self.

 Take a moment to dig deeper into a specific guilt-triggering event from your past. What values or beliefs were challenged? What can you learn from this situation?

_____

_____

_____

_____

_____

 ## *Forgiveness*

Forgiveness doesn't always mean forgiving others; it can also mean forgiving yourself. Accept that you're not perfect, and you will make mistakes. Forgiving yourself is a crucial step in healing and growth.

 Reflect on a situation where you need to forgive yourself. Write a forgiveness letter to yourself, acknowledging your imperfections and granting yourself the gift of forgiveness.

I forgive myself for:

_____

_____

_____

_____

_____

_____

Seek Support

Don't hesitate to seek support from friends, family, or anyone you trust. Talking about your guilt with someone you trust can provide valuable insights and emotional relief.

> **Reach out to a trusted friend or family member and have an open conversation about a recent guilt-triggering event. Share your feelings. Write down what you took away from their perspective.**

_____

_____

_____

_____

_____

Take Action

Guilt often arises from a sense of powerlessness. To transform guilt into growth, take constructive actions that align with your values and help you make amends, if necessary.

> **Write down one small action you can take to address the source of your guilt. It could be an apology, a commitment to change, or a kind gesture toward someone.**

_____

_____

_____

Several studies suggest that acknowledging and working through guilt can lead to improved emotional well-being and reduced symptoms of anxiety and depression (Keng et al., 2011). These findings highlight the potential benefits of embracing your guilt.

As you explore your own shadow work, it's essential to remember that guilt, though intimidating at times, serves as a valuable tool for self-discovery and personal growth. You can harness this emotion to facilitate your transformation, leading you toward healing and enhanced self-regulation.

Healing Shame

Shame is that feeling deep within us that tells us we are fundamentally flawed, unworthy, or unlovable. It often stems from early life experiences, societal expectations, and even cultural norms. It's essential to understand that shame is a natural human emotion, and everyone experiences it to some degree. However, it becomes problematic when it festers in the shadows of our psyche, affecting our self-esteem, relationships, and overall well-being.

Why shame is not helpful:

◆ **It's paralyzing:** Shame can keep us stuck in a cycle of self-criticism and self-doubt, preventing personal growth.

◆ **It's isolating:** When we feel ashamed, we tend to hide our true selves, disconnecting from others and hindering genuine connections.

◆ **It hinders self-acceptance:** True self-acceptance requires acknowledging our shadows and working through shame to embrace all aspects of ourselves.

Exercises

> Write down instances when you've felt shame and explore the underlying beliefs and triggers. Challenge these negative thoughts with self-affirmations.

_____

_____

_____

> Write down five affirmations that can reinforce your self-worth and self-acceptance. Repeat them daily to reprogram your subconscious mind.

1. _____

_____

2. _____

_____

3. _____

_____

4. _____

_____

5. _____

_____

Remember, healing shame is a process, and it's okay to take small steps. You are brave for embarking on this journey. Each day, you'll move closer to the peace and healing you deserve.

Examine the Ego

Our ego is like a protective shield that we all have. It's the part of us that forms our identity, helps us navigate the world, and keeps us safe from harm. It's essential for our survival, but sometimes it can become too dominant, leading to a range of negative emotions and behaviors.

Exercise: Ego Awareness

 Take a few moments once a day for a week to reflect on moments when you felt strong emotions. Write down the situations and try to identify which emotions were triggered by your ego. This will help you become more aware of its influence on your life.

	Situation that triggered a strong emotional reaction	Emotions Triggered
Monday		
Tuesday		
Wednesday		
Thursday		
Friday		
Saturday		
Sunday		

Mastering your ego doesn't mean eliminating it but rather understanding and balancing it. Here are some practical tips to help you on this journey:

◆ **Self-reflection:** Set aside time each day for introspection. Continue to journal your thoughts and feelings to gain insights into your ego's patterns.

◆ **Mindfulness meditation:** Practice mindfulness to observe your thoughts without judgment. This can help you detach from your ego's narratives.

◆ **Seek feedback:** Ask those closest to you for honest feedback about your ego-driven behaviors. This external perspective can be eye-opening.

◆ **Cultivate humility:** Recognize that you're not perfect and your ego has flaws. Embrace your imperfections as opportunities for growth.

◆ **Engage in self-compassion:** You need to start treating yourself exactly as you treat those you love.

 Ego-Balancing Journal

 Write down instances when you noticed your ego at play, and reflect on how you can balance it with humility and self-compassion.

Being a Mirror to Ourselves

It is believed that the best way to understand your shadow is by analyzing your most difficult relationships. Let's explore how the people around us can reflect our innermost struggles and offer valuable insights into our shadow selves.

 Begin by making a list of the people with whom you've had challenging or emotionally charged interactions. These could be family members, friends, coworkers, or even acquaintances.

For each person on your list, jot down the emotions or reactions they provoke in you. Are they making you feel angry, anxious, or insecure? What are the recurring patterns or themes in these relationships?

Names	Emotions they provoke in you

Explore your triggers by asking yourself why these interactions affect you so deeply. What is it about their behavior or words that hit a nerve? Are there any past experiences or wounds that may be contributing to your reactions?

_____

_____

_____

_____

Recognize that these challenging relationships are mirrors reflecting your own unresolved issues or unacknowledged emotions. As you dig deeper, you'll uncover aspects of your shadow self that you may not have been aware of before.

Approach this process with self-compassion. Remember that shadow work is about healing and growth, not self-blame. Embrace your shadows as a part of your whole self.

Interactive Element

 ### *Family Tree Exercise*

Examine your family tree

 Make a family tree of your two sets of grandparents, all of your aunts and uncles, and your parents because they're the generations above you whose attributes—good and bad— might be in you.

The Generations Above You

Mom's Family Tree

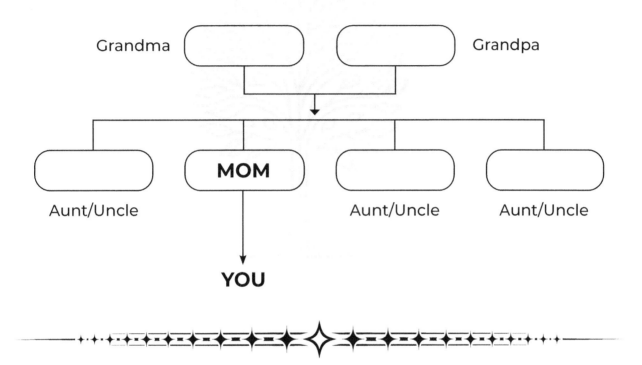

Dad's Family Tree

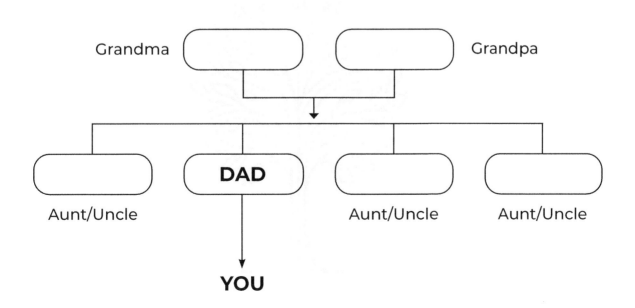

Now, you need to take a good look at all the qualities that you notice within your family and ask yourself which of those you notice within you.

Look for family behavioral patterns and write down what you uncover.

Family Member's Name	Qualities They Have That You Notice Within You

Exercise: Talk to Your Inner Child

Find a childhood photo that resonates with you.

 Talk to them and ask them what they need now or what they needed back then.

Write down what you think those answers would be.

Exercise: People as Mirrors

Think of someone who bothers you, and reflect on what it is about that person that might also be within you.

What is it about this person that I don't like?

Do I find that I have some of those same traits sometimes?

_____

_____

_____

_____

_____

_____

_____

_____

What makes it so difficult to be around them?

_____

_____

_____

_____

_____

_____

_____

_____

When that person is around me, what parts of me do I notice brighten up?

And how do I feel about that part of myself?'

In this chapter, we've delved into more advanced concepts of shadow work, exploring the intricacies of our hidden aspects with depth and courage. You've journeyed through the labyrinth of your psyche, uncovering layers of your shadow self that may have been concealed for years. As you continue on this path of self-discovery, it's important to acknowledge the progress you've made and the insights you've gained.

Now, as we move forward into the next chapter, we'll explore the vital process of integrating your shadow self. This is where you can expect real transformation to happen. Integrating your shadow isn't about erasing or denying these aspects but embracing them as a part of your whole self. It's about harnessing the wisdom and strength that lies within your shadow and using it to propel your personal growth.

So, as you turn the page and embark on the next stage of your journey, be prepared to merge your newfound awareness with your conscious self. By integrating your shadow, you'll find a sense of wholeness and authenticity that can lead to a more fulfilling and empowered life. Embrace this next chapter with an open heart and an open mind, for it holds the key to unlocking your true potential.

CHAPTER 7
INTEGRATING YOUR
SHADOW SELF

Integrating Your Shadow Self

> *If you don't accept yourself, you can't transcend yourself and the world: first, you need to increase your awareness, then you need to accept what you learn, then you need to take action.*
> *–Oli Anderson*

Your shadow self is not broken. It's not a problem to be fixed but rather a facet of your complete self waiting to be acknowledged and integrated. Just like every part of you, your shadow self has its own stories, experiences, and wisdom to offer.

In this chapter, we'll explore the idea that some aspects of your shadow self are not inherently negative or destructive. Instead, they are there to teach you something valuable about yourself. By understanding and integrating these aspects, you can become a more whole and authentic version of yourself.

Think of your shadow self as a puzzle piece that's been hidden away for far too long. As we gently uncover and fit these pieces into the mosaic of your self-awareness, you'll find that the picture of who you truly are becomes clearer and more beautiful than ever before.

So, let's start this journey together with an open heart and a willingness to embrace all that makes you, you. We'll explore practical exercises, thoughtful reflections, and supportive guidance to help you integrate your shadow self in a safe and inviting space.

By the end of this chapter, you'll see that your shadow self isn't something to be feared but something to be welcomed as an integral part of your journey toward personal growth and self-acceptance.

What Is Shadow Self-Integration

At its core, shadow integration is about bringing the hidden parts of yourself into the light of your awareness. Imagine these hidden parts as the shadows that exist just beyond the reach of a flashlight. These shadows, often referred to as your "shadow self," contain both positive and negative aspects of your personality, and they're elements that you've pushed away or denied for various reasons.

Think of it this way: Imagine a coin with two sides. One side represents the traits that society, your family, or your peers have labeled as "bad" or "immoral." These might include things like anger, sexuality, or untamed impulses. These traits were likely suppressed because they didn't align with the values of the people around you.

Now, flip that coin over, and you'll find the traits that were pushed into the shadows even though they are positive and life-promoting. These might include your assertiveness, creativity, competitiveness, or ambition. They were hidden away because they may have been seen as a threat or were simply not encouraged.

So, when we talk about shadow self-integration, we mean the process of acknowledging and embracing both sides of the coin—the parts of you that have been repressed, whether they are considered "good" or "bad" by others. It's about making peace with all these aspects, not to achieve perfection but to move toward wholeness.

Carl Jung emphasized that our goal should be to become whole, not perfect. The journey to becoming a complete and fulfilled person involves integrating these elements of our psyche that have been hidden away for too long *(How to Integrate Your Shadow–the Dark Side Is Unrealized Potential, 2020)*.

By doing so, you're not only healing the wounds caused by repressing certain traits but also unlocking your hidden potential. Your greater character, your more effective approach to life, lies in embracing your entire self. As you bring your shadow self into the light, you'll experience a profound sense of freedom and vitality that comes from living authentically *(Shadow Integration 101, 2019)*.

Integrating Shadow Work into Daily Life

Mindful Excercise: Practice It As Often As You Can

Mindfulness is a powerful tool for integrating shadow work into your daily life. It requires you to be present in the moment and notice your thoughts and emotions without judgment.

 Find a quiet space, sit comfortably, and focus on your breath for a few minutes. Be mindful of thoughts or emotions that you feel without trying to change them. Write down your observations.

_____

_____

_____

_____

_____

_____

_____

Exercise: Pay Attention to Your Triggers

As you move deeper into shadow work, you may uncover memories and emotions that trigger feelings of shame or discomfort. Recognizing these triggers is essential for growth.

 Use this space as a trigger journal. Whenever you experience a trigger, jot down the situation, your feelings, and any memories associated with it. This will give you the ability to notice any patterns in your shadow.

Triggers	Feelings & Memories Evoked

Exercise: Pay Attention to the Feelings in Your Body

Emotions often manifest physically. Pay attention to bodily sensations, as they can provide valuable insights into your shadow self.

> I would like you to find a spot where you feel safe and comfortable. Gently close your eyes if you are okay doing so. Next, inhale with three deep breaths and slowly scan your body from head to toe. Note any areas of tension or discomfort and record them in your workbook.

_____

_____

_____

_____

Exercise: Take Deep Breaths as You Process Painful Memories

When you encounter painful memories or emotions during shadow work, deep breathing can help you stay grounded and regulate your emotions.

> Create a breathing break routine. When you feel overwhelmed by difficult emotions, take a few minutes to sit quietly and focus on your breath. Inhale deeply for a count of four, hold for four, and exhale for four. Repeat until you feel more centered.

Exercise: Take Note of Thought Patterns and Habits

Shadow work often reveals recurring thought patterns and habits that have been holding you back. Identifying these is a key step in personal growth.

 Keep a thought and habit log in your workbook. Throughout the day, jot down any thoughts or behaviors that you notice are unhelpful or self-sabotaging. This awareness will enable you to work on transforming these patterns over time.

Negative Thoughts & Habits Log

1. _____

2. _____

3. _____

4. _____

5. _____

6. _____

7. _____

8. _____

9. _____

10. _____

11. _____

12. _____

Research has shown that incorporating mindfulness practices into daily life can lead to reduced stress, improved emotional regulation, and enhanced overall well-being (Keng et al., 2011). Additionally, studies on trauma-focused therapy emphasize the importance of recognizing triggers and addressing bodily sensations to heal from past traumatic experiences (Sweeney et al., 2018).

Sheila's Story

Sheila's life had always seemed picture-perfect on the surface. To her friends and family, she appeared confident, successful, and full of energy. However, behind her radiant smile, Sheila grappled with an overwhelming sense of anxiety, persistent guilt, and a never-ending feeling of emotional exhaustion. Every day felt like a battle, and she often found herself overwhelmed by a wide range of unwanted emotions, from anxiety and fear to deep sadness and mental exhaustion.

One evening, while scrolling through social media, Sheila came across a post about shadow work. The concept intrigued her, and as she delved into articles and videos, she realized that this might be the missing piece in her journey toward self-discovery and healing. She felt apprehensive but also curious, sensing that shadow work could provide her with the tools she needed to regain control over her emotions and life.

Sheila began her shadow work journey with cautious optimism. She started by exploring her past, reflecting on her childhood experiences and early memories. It wasn't always easy, as some of these memories were painful and brought up intense emotions. But she persevered, determined to understand the root causes of her anxiety and guilt.

As she delved deeper into her shadow, Sheila discovered triggers she hadn't recognized before. Certain situations or comments would provoke intense feelings of shame or insecurity. Instead of pushing these emotions away, she decided to confront them head-on. Sheila created a "Trigger Journal" in her shadow work workbook, noting down each trigger, the feelings it evoked, and any associated memories. This practice helped her identify patterns in her shadow self, providing valuable insights into her emotional landscape.

Sheila also paid close attention to her body's reactions during her shadow work sessions. She noticed that her shoulders would tense up, and her heart would race when she revisited painful memories. To address this, she incorporated a daily "Body Scan" practice. Sitting quietly, she closed her eyes, took deep breaths, and mentally scanned her body from head to toe. This exercise allowed her to release physical tension and remain present in the moment.

One of the most significant breakthroughs for Sheila was recognizing her recurring thought patterns and habits. Through her shadow work, she discovered that she often engaged in negative self-talk and self-sabotaging behaviors. To address this, she maintained a "Thought and Habit Log" in her workbook. Throughout the day, she recorded any detrimental thoughts or behaviors she noticed. Over time, this awareness empowered her to challenge and transform these patterns into more positive and self-affirming ones.

As months passed, Sheila's consistent commitment to shadow work and daily integration paid off. She found herself more in control of her emotions, and her anxiety and guilt began to lose their grip on her. Sheila started to experience moments of inner peace and emotional balance that she had never thought possible. Her smile became even more radiant, but this time, it was genuine and reflected the newfound authenticity and self-acceptance she had discovered through her shadow work journey.

Sheila's story serves as an inspiring example of the power of shadow work and daily integration. It's a reminder that, no matter how daunting the journey may seem, with dedication, self-compassion, and the right tools, you can find your way to a brighter, more fulfilling life.

Remember, integrating shadow work into your daily life is a gradual process. Be patient and compassionate with yourself. The more you practice these strategies and activities, the more in control you'll feel and the closer you'll get to the personal growth and self-healing you desire.

Stay committed to your journey, and the light you shed on your shadow self will illuminate a path toward a brighter, more authentic you.

Visualization

Visualization can be a potent technique in your shadow work meditation arsenal. It helps you create a safe and inviting space to connect with your inner self, and it allows you to explore your shadow without fear or judgment. Let's dive into a visualization exercise designed to help you integrate your shadow self.

 ## *Exercise: Shadow Integration Visualization*

Begin by finding a quiet and comfortable space where you won't be disturbed. Imagine this place as your sacred sanctuary, a safe haven where you can be yourself.

> **Before we get focused, I want you to move your thoughts to one particular area of your life where you've been struggling. This could be a recurring issue that brings you pain, anger, or sadness. Write it down. This is the shadow you'll be working with today.**

- ◆ Now, close your eyes and take three deep, slow breaths. With each breath, release any tension or apprehension you may be feeling.

- ◆ Invite your shadow to step forward into your sacred space. Pay attention to its appearance and form. It may take on a physical shape or represent itself in another way.

◆ Ask your shadow when and how it was created. Request that it shows you the moment in your life when it first emerged. Allow yourself to go back in time, even if it stirs up intense emotions.

◆ Have a conversation with your shadow. Ask it what it needs from you at this moment to facilitate growth and healing. Take mental notes of its responses; these will serve as your action items.

◆ Take a moment to express your love and gratitude to your shadow. Acknowledge the lessons it has taught you. Visualize it becoming smaller and smaller until it fits in the palm of your hand.

◆ Place your hand over your heart and feel your shadow integrating into your entire being. It's no longer a fragmented part of you but a stronger, integrated aspect.

◆ Take three more deep breaths while sitting in your sacred space. Allow this newfound integration to settle within you.

◆ When you're ready, open your eyes. Write down how you feel in the area of your life you were focusing on earlier. Do you feel more at peace, lighter, and more confident?

_____

_____

_____

_____

This visualization exercise serves as a bridge between your conscious and shadow self. It helps you confront and understand the hidden aspects of yourself that have been causing emotional turmoil. By integrating your shadow self with love and acceptance, you empower yourself to move forward on your path of personal growth and healing.

Reflecting on Your Progress in Shadow Work

One of the most important aspects of shadow work is acknowledging and celebrating your progress. This is a key step to keep your motivation high and build your self-confidence. Here's how you can do it:

◆ **Keep a shadow work journal:**

- Create a dedicated journal where you can document your experiences, insights, and milestones.

- Write down moments when you confronted a shadow aspect successfully or gained a deeper understanding of yourself.

◆ **Set small goals:**

- Break down your shadow work into manageable goals.

- Celebrate each time you achieve a goal, no matter how small it may seem.

◆ **Reward yourself:**

- Treat yourself to something special when you reach a significant milestone.

- This can be as simple as enjoying your favorite meal, taking a relaxing bath, or going for a nature walk.

◆ **Share your achievements:**

- Don't be shy about sharing your progress with a supportive friend or a trusted therapist.

- Their encouragement can be a powerful motivator and reminder of how far you've come.

Dealing with Plateaus and Challenges

It's natural to encounter plateaus and challenges on your shadow work journey. These moments can be frustrating, but they are also opportunities for growth. Here's how to navigate them:

- **Accept plateaus as part of the process:**

  - Understand that plateaus are common and can be indicative of deeper work ahead.

  - Use this time to reflect and reassess your approach.

- **Don't give up when challenges arise:**

  - When you encounter difficult emotions or resistance, don't let it discourage you.

  - Take a step back, breathe, and remember that this is an essential part of your healing journey.

- **Practice self-compassion:**

  - Be gentle with yourself during challenging times.

  - Self-compassion allows you to acknowledge your struggles without self-criticism.

Adjusting Your Approach Based on Progress

As you make progress in your shadow work, it's essential to adjust your approach to ensure continued growth and healing.

◆ **Regularly review your goals:**

- Periodically revisit your initial goals and assess if they still align with your evolving understanding of yourself.

- Adjust them as needed to stay aligned with your current needs.

◆ **Expand your toolkit:**

- Explore new shadow work techniques and practices.

- Experiment with meditation, journaling, dream analysis, or therapy to deepen your self-discovery.

◆ **Celebrate your evolving self:**

- Recognize that your progress is a testament to your strength and resilience.

- Celebrate not only the changes you've made but also your willingness to grow.

◆ **Stay patient and persistent:**

- Remember that shadow work is an ongoing process.

- Embrace the journey and trust that it will lead you to a place of greater self-awareness and healing.

Interactive Element: Practical Tools For Tracking Progress

I wanted to offer five of the top tools for tracking progress while on this journey. Writing in a journal is helpful, but as busy as we can get, having an app at our disposal can be a huge help. Let's review the ones people seem to love the most:

1 Shadow work App—Apple Store:

- This dedicated app is a gem for anyone on their shadow work journey. It's designed to provide you with guidance, support, and structured exercises to help you explore and integrate your shadow aspects.

- One reviewer beautifully summed it up: "Thank you for teaching me how to come from love and not fear." This app can truly help you shift from a place of fear to one of self-compassion and love.

2 Day One Journaling App—mobile and desktop:

- If you prefer the written word, the Day One Journaling App is your perfect companion. It's not just about writing down your thoughts; it's about recording your daily reflections and insights.

- As one user passionately shared, "This is my favorite app. I use it every day if 72,000 words weren't telling enough." It's a testament to how this app can help you dig deep and discover your inner thoughts and emotions.

3 Journey: Journal App:

- Journey is more than just a journaling app; it's a holistic self-improvement tool. It offers audio options, making it accessible even on the go.

- What sets it apart is its mood-tracking feature, allowing you to monitor your emotional state throughout your shadow work journey. Additionally, you can opt into coaching programs on self-confidence, boundary setting, and mindfulness, making it an all-encompassing choice for your self-growth journey.

4 Penzu:

- For those concerned about privacy, Penzu is the answer. It's a secure online journaling platform available on iOS and Android. Your entries are protected with password security, ensuring your thoughts remain private.

- Customization options and the ability to add photos to your entries make Penzu suitable for recording your shadow work experiences in a visually engaging way.

5 Evernote:

- Evernote is a versatile note-taking app that can be easily adapted for journaling. Its cross-platform support means you can access your entries from anywhere.

- Evernote is especially helpful for shadow work because of its robust search functionality and tagging system. These features allow you to organize and easily locate your entries, making it an excellent choice for reflection and review.

Choose the tool that resonates with you the most, whether it's an app designed specifically for shadow work or a versatile journaling platform. These tools will not only help you track your progress but also provide a safe and organized space for your self-exploration journey. Remember, the journey is unique to you, and these tools are here to support you every step of the way.

In this chapter, we've explored the profound concept of shadow integration, the process of accepting and embracing your shadow side. By doing so, you've taken a courageous step to become a fully whole being, where your shadow and light coexist harmoniously.

Accepting your shadow is not about denying your light or succumbing to your darkness. It's about recognizing that you are a complex and multifaceted being. Just as the sun casts both light and shadows, so do you. When you integrate your shadow aspects, you unlock a profound sense of freedom, joy, and wholeness.

With your shadow work journey underway, you're poised to step into the next and final chapter. Here, you'll explore hope, motivation, and inspiration to continue your transformative journey. You've already come so far, and your inner light is ready to shine brighter than ever before.

Stay curious, stay compassionate, and most importantly, stay committed to your personal growth. The path ahead may have challenges, but it's also illuminated by the brilliance of your own light.

CHAPTER 8

CONSCIOUSLY LIVING IN THE LIGHT

Consciously Living in the Light

> " *Your life will be transformed when you make peace with your shadow. The caterpillar will become a breathtakingly beautiful butterfly. You will no longer have to pretend to be someone you're not. You will no longer have to prove you're good enough.*
> **–Debbie Ford**

You've come a long way from the beginning of this workbook, and your commitment to exploring your shadow self has been truly remarkable. As we engage in this final chapter, I want you to take a moment to acknowledge the courage it took to confront your hidden aspects, the parts of yourself that you may have long ignored or denied.

In this final chapter, we'll explore what it means to consciously live in the light. It's the culmination of your efforts, the point where your shadow and your conscious self can come together in harmony. It's about applying the lessons you've learned in your daily life, using your newfound self-awareness to navigate challenges, and building a brighter, more fulfilling future.

But before we dive into the practical aspects of consciously living in the light, I want you to pause and reflect on the progress you've made. Always be mindful of your victories. Celebrate all of them. You've faced your fears, acknowledged your pain, and taken crucial steps toward self-healing and personal growth.

As you move forward, you'll continue to uncover new layers of your shadow and integrate them into your conscious self. It's a path filled with ups and downs, but each step brings you closer to a brighter, more authentic version of yourself.

So, as we embark on this final chapter, let hope, motivation, and inspiration fill your heart. You've already proven your strength and resilience, and the future holds endless possibilities for you. By consciously living in the light, you'll not only benefit yourself but also the people around you. Your newfound self-awareness will shine as a beacon of positivity, and your journey will inspire others to embark on their own path of self-discovery and healing.

When Are We Done?

So you might be wondering, "How will I know when I'm done? Is there an endpoint to this journey?" The short answer is no There's no finish line in shadow work because personal growth is an ongoing process. However, there are some clear signs that can help you recognize your progress.

 ## *Exercise: Emotional Resilience*

One significant indicator of healing your shadow is that your emotional responses become more balanced and resilient. The things that used to trigger intense reactions in you may no longer have that power. You'll notice that you can handle difficult situations with greater composure.

 Write down a list of situations, people, or events that used to trigger strong emotional reactions in you. Now, reflect on how you respond to them today.

Triggering Situations	How did you respond TODAY?

Have you noticed any changes? How do you feel about your progress?

 ## *Exercise: Less Projection*

When you're deep into shadow work, you often project your own unresolved issues onto others. As you heal, you'll find that you're less likely to blame or judge others for things that are actually about you. Your relationships become more harmonious and authentic.

Recall a recent conflict or disagreement you had with someone. Write down how you reacted. Were you quick to blame them, or did you pause to reflect on your own feelings and reactions? Analyze how you handled the situation and how you might approach it differently now.

Exercise: Improved Self-Awareness

The more you explore your shadow, the more you understand yourself. You become more in tune with your thoughts, emotions, and behaviors. This heightened self-awareness allows you to make conscious choices rather than reacting on autopilot.

Keep a journal for a week where you jot down your thoughts, feelings, and actions in different situations. At the end of the week, review your journal and identify any patterns or triggers you notice. How can this awareness help you grow?

Monday

The thoughts and feelings I had today are_____

_____

_____

_____

Actions I did or didn't take today are_____

_____

_____

_____

Tuesday

The thoughts and feelings I had today are_____

_____

_____

_____

Actions I did or didn't take today are_____

_____

_____

_____

Wednesday

The thoughts and feelings I had today are_____

_____

_____

_____

Actions I did or didn't take today are_____

_____

_____

_____

Thursday

The thoughts and feelings I had today are_____

_____

_____

_____

Actions I did or didn't take today are_____

_____

_____

_____

Friday

The thoughts and feelings I had today are_____

_____

_____

_____

Actions I did or didn't take today are_____

_____

_____

_____

Saturday

The thoughts and feelings I had today are_____

_____

_____

_____

Actions I did or didn't take today are_____

_____

_____

_____

Sunday

The thoughts and feelings I had today are_____

_____

_____

_____

Actions I did or didn't take today are_____

_____

_____

_____

Review your self-awareness journal and identify any patterns or triggers you notice. How can this awareness help you grow?

_____

_____

_____

_____

_____

_____

Exercise: Forgiveness and Compassion

Healing your shadow often involves forgiving yourself for past mistakes and embracing self-compassion. When you find it easier to forgive yourself and others, it's a sign that you're making progress.

 Reflect on a mistake or regret from your past. How do you feel about it now? Can you find it in yourself to forgive yourself for that moment? Write a letter of forgiveness to yourself or to someone who may have hurt you.

A study found that individuals who engage in shadow work and self-exploration report decreased levels of anxiety and depression and improved self-esteem over time (Mayer, 2023).

Mitchell's Story

Mitchell, like many of us, had his fair share of inner turmoil. He struggled with intense anxiety that often left him feeling paralyzed. Every day seemed like a battle, and he longed for a sense of control over his emotions. His heart raced, his palms sweated, and his thoughts spiraled into a never-ending loop of worry.

The idea of shadow work initially filled Mitchell with trepidation. He knew it meant delving into the depths of his psyche, confronting buried emotions, and addressing past traumas. But he also knew that something had to change. He couldn't continue to live in the shadow of his anxiety.

With determination, Mitchell took the first step on this daunting path. He committed himself to the process, understanding that it wouldn't be easy, but it was necessary for his personal growth and healing.

As the weeks turned into months, Mitchell began to notice significant changes in his life. His anxiety attacks, which used to be a daily ordeal, became less frequent and less severe. The relentless grip of fear began to loosen.

One pivotal moment occurred during a family gathering, an event that had always triggered crippling anxiety. Mitchell had a history of feeling inadequate, stemming from his childhood experiences and a deep-seated fear of abandonment.

But this time, something was different. As he stood amidst the chatter of relatives and the clinking of dishes, Mitchell felt an unexpected calm wash over him. He realized that he was no longer overwhelmed by his anxiety. The same situation that had once sent him into a panic had lost its power.

It was a powerful moment of realization. Mitchell had, through his dedicated shadow work, unearthed and confronted the roots of his anxiety. He had explored the shadows of inadequacy and the fear of abandonment that had haunted him for so long. By doing so, he had taken back control over his emotions and his life.

He realized that his triggers, which had once held him hostage, no longer had the same grip on him. It was a liberating feeling that brought tears of joy and relief to his eyes.

Mitchell's journey, much like your own, is a testament to the transformative power of shadow work. It shows that with dedication, self-compassion, and the willingness to face your inner demons, you can overcome even the most profound inner struggles.

How To Get Back On Track

Now that you have come this far in acknowledging what your shadow self is and how to integrate it, how will you know when it is taking over? What signs will show you that you're reacting or making bad decisions based on your shadow self, that part of you rooted in the past? Once you recognize this is happening, how do you change course and get back on track?

Let's review some caution signs that your shadow side may be taking over:

◆ **Intense emotional reactions:** Even after doing all of this work, it can be normal to find yourself experiencing strong emotions like anger, anxiety, or sadness that seem out of proportion to the situation. Just be mindful that this is your shadow self.

◆ **Repeated patterns:** You once again notice recurring patterns in your life, such as consistently attracting the same types of unhealthy relationships or encountering the same obstacles. After doing this work, you can recognize this is your shadow self.

◆ **Projection:** You might frequently find yourself once again judging or reacting strongly to certain qualities or behaviors in others. You understand now these might actually be reflections of your unacknowledged traits.

◆ **Self-sabotage:** You may engage in self-destructive behaviors or habits that hinder your personal growth, like procrastination, substance abuse, or excessive self-criticism. Be mindful that this is your shadow self.

 ## *Exercise: Shadow Self Check-In*

Here are some key questions to ask yourself daily to help you gain better control over your shadow self.

 Ask yourself if this choice, decision, or reaction is helping or harming me or others. Take a moment to reflect on your decisions and actions. Write down whether they align with your values and serve your well-being. If you catch yourself acting in a way that's harmful, pause and write down why think you're making that choice.

What emotions am I feeling, and why? Regularly check in with your emotions. Write down your answers to the following: Am I feeling angry, anxious, or sad? Try to trace these emotions back to their source. Are they linked to past experiences or suppressed feelings?

 Am I projecting my own unacknowledged qualities? When you find yourself strongly reacting to someone else's behavior, consider whether you might be projecting your own suppressed traits onto them. When the situation is resolved, take some time to write down your thoughts. Were you able to see your shadow self in your reaction, and if so, how did you handle it? This awareness can help you reclaim those aspects of yourself.

Ivy's Story

Meet Ivy, a young woman who has been grappling with chronic anxiety for most of her life. She had embarked on the challenging path of shadow work, determined to unearth the buried aspects of her personality and heal her emotional wounds. As she moved into her shadow, Ivy began to discover the roots of her anxiety, which were deeply intertwined with her childhood experiences.

Ivy's shadow work was a path marked by perseverance and self-discovery. She spent countless hours in self-reflection and introspection, slowly bringing her shadow self into the light. She unearthed long-buried memories of her parents' turbulent divorce and the emotional neglect she had suffered during her formative years.

However, despite her progress, Ivy still faced moments when her past would resurface, and her anxiety would impose itself on her current relationships. It was in these moments that she would become frustrated and wonder why she had bothered with all the hard work on herself in the first place.

One day, Ivy found herself in a heated argument with her partner over something seemingly trivial. Her heart raced, her palms became sweaty, and she felt an overwhelming urge to lash out, just as she had done in the past. In that moment, Ivy's old patterns seemed to be reasserting themselves.

But Ivy had developed a set of strategies to identify her shadow self and regain her balance when such situations arose. She took a deep breath and asked herself the key questions she had learned during her shadow work journey:

 ### *"What Emotions Am I Feeling, and Why?"*

Ivy recognized that the intense anger she was experiencing was a familiar defense mechanism. It was a way her shadow self used to protect her from feeling vulnerable, just as she had felt vulnerable during her parents' divorce.

"Am I Reacting or Responding?"

She realized that she was reacting impulsively rather than responding thoughtfully. Ivy's shadow self was trying to protect her, but it was doing so in an outdated and harmful way.

 ## *"Is This Choice or Act Helping or Harming Me or Others?"*

Ivy acknowledged that her outburst was harming both her and her partner. This realization helped her step back from the brink of the argument and choose a more constructive path.

Through her shadow work, Ivy cultivated self-awareness and a toolbox of coping strategies. She knew how to recognize when her shadow self was reacting, and she had learned to respond in healthier ways. Ivy reached out to her partner, apologized for her behavior, and explained that her anxiety had momentarily taken control.

Over time, Ivy's dedication to shadow work paid off. She found herself having fewer and less intense moments of anxiety-driven reactions. Her relationships improved, and she felt a growing sense of peace within herself.

Ivy's journey was a testament to the power of shadow work and self-awareness. While her shadow self occasionally resurfaced, Ivy had the tools and resilience to navigate those moments and continue her path of healing and growth. Her story inspired others to embark on their own journey of self-discovery, knowing that transformation was possible, one step at a time.

Underlying Fear

In this section, we'll explore how fear underlies many of our unhelpful choices and thoughts. By exploring this topic, you'll gain clearer insights into your shadow self and continue the path to a life of growth and self-healing.

Fear is a primal emotion deeply ingrained in our human psyche. It's a natural response that has both a universal biochemical aspect and a highly individualized emotional component (Fritscher, 2023). Understanding fear can help us unlock the power of shadow work.

When we talk about fear, we need to understand that it is made up of two different reactions when we perceive a threat (Fritscher, 2023):

Biochemical reaction to fear: When we think there is a threat, our bodies experience a set of physical reactions. These include sweating, an increased heart rate, and a surge of adrenaline that makes us hyper-alert. This physical response is often called "fight or flight," where your body prepares itself to either confront the danger or escape from it. This reaction is a product of evolution and plays a vital role in our survival.

Emotional response to fear: The physical reaction to fear is pretty consistent among most of us, but the emotional response is highly personalized. Interestingly, fear triggers some of the same chemical reactions in our brains that positive emotions like happiness and excitement do. This is why some of us find certain fear-inducing situations exhilarating, such as jumping out of planes or axe throwing.

On the flip side, there are those who have a negative reaction to fear and actively avoid fear-inducing situations. For them, fear can be paralyzing and cause distress. The experience of fear, whether positive or negative, largely depends on the person and their life experiences.

So, how does fear play into shadow work? Well, fear often acts as a barrier that prevents us from exploring our shadow selves. It's the voice that says, "Don't go there; it's too painful" or "You're not ready to face that aspect of yourself." This fear can manifest in various ways, from self-doubt to procrastination and avoidance.

Exercise: Overcoming Fear

Take a moment to reflect on what specific fears might be hindering your self-discovery journey. Write them down. Awareness is the first step.

1. _____

_____

2. _____

_____

3. _____

_____

4. _____

_____

5. _____

_____

Be gentle with yourself. Recognize that fear is a natural response, and it's okay to feel it. Embrace self-compassion as you navigate your fears.

Start small. Begin with less intimidating aspects of your shadow self before delving into deeper layers. This gradual exposure can build your confidence.

Imagine a safe and nurturing space where you can explore your shadow without judgment or harm. Visualization can help you feel more at ease.

Noticing Fear

So, let's get started on understanding fear, one of the emotions that often hides in our shadows.

Fear is a powerful and complex emotion. It can manifest in various ways and often lurks beneath many of the negative feelings—anxiety, guilt, sadness, and more. By shining a light on your fears, you can start to regain control over your emotions and find a path toward healing.

Let's break down fear into some common categories and types:

◆ **Survival fear:** This is the most primal fear, rooted in our survival instincts. It includes the fear of physical harm, danger, or death. For example, fear of heights, spiders, or loud noises.

◆ **Emotional fear:** These fears are related to our emotional well-being. They can include fear of rejection, abandonment, or loneliness. Emotional fears often underlie issues like low self-esteem or social anxiety.

◆ **Fear of the unknown:** This fear revolves around uncertainty and the future. It can manifest as anxiety about what might happen, fear of change, or fear of the unfamiliar.

◆ **Fear of failure:** Many people grapple with the fear of not being good enough, fear of making mistakes, or fear of disappointing others. This fear can lead to perfectionism and self-doubt.

◆ **Fear of vulnerability:** This fear is tied to showing your true self to others. It can make you put up emotional walls, afraid of being hurt if you let people in. It often masks deeper insecurities.

Understanding the types of fear is just the first step. Now, let's explore what might be hiding beneath these fears:

◆ **Past trauma:** Sometimes, your fears are rooted in past traumatic experiences. They act as a defense mechanism to protect you from reliving those painful moments.

◆ **Limiting beliefs:** Negative beliefs about yourself or the world can fuel your fears. Identifying and challenging these beliefs is crucial for growth.

◆ **Unmet needs:** Fear can arise when your core emotional needs aren't being met, such as the need for love, acceptance, or safety.

◆ **Repressed emotions:** Fear often conceals other emotions like anger, sadness, or shame. Your shadow self might be using fear as a shield to avoid dealing with these deeper feelings.

Fear Exercises

 Create a fear journal and write down instances when you felt afraid. Try to categorize them into the types of fear we discussed. For each fear, reflect on what might be underlying it.

Instances You Felt Afraid	Type of Fear (from the list above)	What Fuels This Fear?

Identify a fear that's been holding you back. Write down the beliefs associated with it. Are these beliefs helping or hindering your growth?

Think back to a specific time when you felt intense fear. Can you recall what exactly was happening in your life at that time? Are there any unprocessed emotions or unmet needs associated with that memory?

Recent studies have shown that acknowledging and confronting your fears can lead to reduced anxiety and improved emotional regulation (Cisler et al., 2009).

Processing Fear: Using Fear as a Catalyst for Growth

Fear is a powerful and natural emotion. It's something we all experience from time to time, and for many, it can feel overwhelming. The good news is that fear is also a valuable tool for self-discovery and growth. It's like a sign pointing to areas of your life that need your attention.

 ### *Exercise: Acknowledge Your Fear*

The first step is to recognize when you're feeling fearful. Take a moment to pause and identify the source of your fear. Is it related to a specific situation, person, or memory? Write it down in your workbook.

 Create a fear journal. Write down instances when you feel fear and include any thoughts or physical sensations that accompany it.

Fear	Physical reactions

Exercise: Breathe Through It

When fear grips you, focus on your breath. Deep, slow breaths can help calm your nervous system and bring you back to the present moment.

> Practice a 5-minute daily breathing exercise. Write down your experiences and any changes in your fear levels.

_____

_____

_____

_____

Exercise: Question Your Fear

Ask yourself why you're feeling this fear. What's the underlying belief or thought that's causing it? Often, our fears are rooted in past experiences or limiting beliefs.

> Write down three of your most common fears and the beliefs associated with them. Challenge these beliefs by seeking evidence to the contrary.

Fear #1:_____

Beliefs associated with that fear	Evidence to the contrary

Fear #2:_____

Beliefs associated with that fear	Evidence to the contrary

Fear #3:_____

Beliefs associated with that fear	Evidence to the contrary

 ## *Exercise: Visualize Fear as a Teacher*

Imagine fear as a wise mentor trying to teach you something important. What lessons might it have for you? This perspective can help you approach fear with curiosity rather than avoidance.

> Visualize a conversation with your fear mentor and write down the lessons or insights it offers.

_____

_____

_____

Strategies for Managing Fear and Anxiety

Fear is like a wall that separates you from the life you desire. If you continually avoid situations that scare you, you'll miss out on valuable experiences and opportunities for growth. Avoidance might temporarily relieve your anxiety, but it often leads to a pattern where anxiety problems intensify over time.

So, how do you break this cycle? By facing your fears head-on. Here's how:

 ## *Set Small, Achievable Goals*

Start small. Identify situations or triggers that make you anxious. Instead of diving into the deep end, set achievable goals to gradually confront your fears. This gradual approach allows you to build confidence and realize that the situation might not be as bad as you expect.

 ## *Exercise: Get to Know Your Fear*

Understanding your fear is essential. Keep an anxiety diary to track your emotions, triggers, and physical sensations when anxiety strikes. This self-awareness will empower you to manage your feelings better.

 Create a list of things that help you cope during anxious moments. This list can be a powerful tool for addressing the underlying beliefs that fuel your anxiety.

1. _____

2. _____

3. _____

4. _____

5. _____

6. _____

7. _____

8. _____

9. _____

10. _____

Share with a Trusted Friend or Family Member

It's common to feel ashamed or silly about your fears and anxieties, but you don't have to face them alone. If you have a trusted friend or family member, confide in them. Talking about your fears can reduce anxiety levels and pave the way for additional support if needed.

Embrace Physical Activity

Exercise is a fantastic way to distract your mind from fear and anxiety. You don't need to run a marathon; even gentle stretches, seated exercises, or a leisurely walk can work wonders. Exercise releases endorphins, the body's natural mood lifters, which can help improve your emotional state.

> **Write down three ways you feel you can move your body.**

1. _____

2. _____

3. _____

Relaxation Techniques

Learning relaxation techniques can help you combat both the mental and physical aspects of fear. Simple practices like deep breathing, envisioning a calming place, or exploring complementary therapies such as massage, yoga, mindfulness, and meditation can provide significant relief.

 Write down three relaxation techniques you believe you can adapt to your daily life.

1. _____

2. _____

3. _____

Nurture Your Body

Your diet can influence anxiety levels. Consume plenty of fruits and vegetables while limiting sugar intake to prevent blood sugar spikes. Minimize your caffeine consumption by reducing tea and coffee, as caffeine can exacerbate anxiety.

 Jot down three things you can do to change your diet to improve your anxiety levels.

1. _____

2. _____

3. _____

Moderate Alcohol Intake

Although some might call it courage, alcohol isn't your ally in managing fear and anxiety. It can intensify anxious feelings and lead to more significant emotional struggles. If you do drink, do so in moderation.

These practical strategies, when combined with self-awareness and the willingness to face your fears, can be powerful tools for managing anxiety and fear as you embark on your shadow work journey.

Jaime's Story

Jaime, much like many of us, faced a constant battle with anxiety and fear. However, instead of confronting these emotions, she turned to unhealthy coping mechanisms to find temporary relief. For instance:

◆ **Anxiety at bedtime:** When the anxiety struck at bedtime, Jaime would reach for a glass, or sometimes three, to help her fall asleep. This reliance on alcohol as a crutch only masked her anxiety temporarily and created a vicious cycle.

◆ **Fear of confrontation at work:** At her job, Jaime had a deep-seated fear of confrontation. This fear held her back from addressing issues and voicing her opinions, even when it meant missing out on significant advancement opportunities. Her avoidance strategy kept her stuck in a job she didn't truly love.

One day, Jaime decided she couldn't continue down this path of self-doubt and anxiety-driven choices. She realized that in order to truly grow and find inner peace, she needed to confront her fears head-on.

Instead of reaching for a glass of alcohol when bedtime anxiety hit, Jaime started practicing relaxation techniques. She used deep breathing exercises and guided imagery to calm her mind. Over time, these techniques became her new bedtime routine, gradually reducing her reliance on alcohol.

Jaime decided to tackle her fear of confrontation at work. She began by setting small, achievable goals. She started by speaking up in team meetings and gradually worked her way up to addressing larger issues. As she saw positive outcomes and received support from colleagues, her confidence grew.

Alongside these changes, Jaime made healthier choices in her life. She started eating better, incorporating more fruits and vegetables into her diet, and reducing her sugar intake. She also decided to drink alcohol in moderation and found that she felt more in control of her emotions as a result.

As Jaime continued to face her fears and adopt healthier coping strategies, her life began to transform. She gained a newfound sense of confidence and self-assuredness. Her relationships improved, both personally and professionally, as she learned to communicate effectively and assertively. Most importantly, Jaime found inner peace that had eluded her for years.

Jaime's journey shows us that with determination, self-awareness, and a willingness to confront our fears, we can break free from the shackles of anxiety and fear. As you embark on your own shadow work, remember that you have the power to transform your life, just like Jaime did. It's a journey of self-discovery and healing, and you're taking the first steps toward a brighter, more peaceful future.

The Antidote to Fear is not Courage—It's Love

In this section, we'll explore a profound truth: the antidote to fear is not courage—it is love. Fear can be an overwhelming and paralyzing emotion, and you've likely felt its grip on your life in various forms.

Let's begin by delving into exercises that will help you embrace the power of love to overcome fear and take charge of your emotional well-being.

 ### Exercise: Self-Compassion

 Write down a list of encouraging and comforting statements about yourself. This is to remind you of your worth. You deserve love and understanding.

1. _____

2. _____

3. _____

4. _____

5. _____

6. _____

7. _____

8. _____

9. _____

10. _____

> List three things you are grateful for. Gratitude can shift your focus from fear to love and abundance.

1. _____

2. _____

3. _____

> Write down three self-care routines that you can use to nurture your body and soul. Whether it's taking a long bath, going for a walk in nature, or simply enjoying a cup of tea, prioritize activities that bring you joy and peace.

1. _____

2. _____

3. _____

Staying Motivated in Your Shadow Work Journey

Motivation fuels your commitment and helps you navigate the challenging moments that will inevitably arise. It's the driving force behind your transformation. Let's review some exercises to help you stay motivated as you continue your shadow work journey.

Exercise: Connect with Nature

Nature can be a powerful ally in your shadow work journey. Spend time outdoors, whether it's a walk in the park, a hike in the woods, or simply sitting in your backyard. Nature has a way of grounding us and providing clarity.

 Dedicate at least 30 minutes each day to connect with nature. Write down your feelings and thoughts during these moments.

Thoughts on Nature Walk #1

_____

_____

_____

_____

_____

Thoughts on Nature Walk #2

_____

_____

_____

_____

_____

Thoughts on Nature Walk #3

 ## Exercise: Explore Creative Expression

Art, writing, music, and other forms of creative expression can be therapeutic. Engage in creative activities that allow you to explore your emotions and experiences in a non-judgmental way.

 Start an art journal, write poetry, or create a playlist of songs that resonate with your journey. Use these outlets to express yourself freely.

 ## Exercise: Seek Guidance from Dreams

Our dreams often hold valuable insights. Keep a dream journal by your bedside and jot down your dreams upon waking. Over time, patterns and symbols may emerge that shed light on your shadow.

 Start a dream journal and record your dreams regularly. Look for recurring themes or symbols and contemplate their significance.

Exercise: Vision Board

I want to invite you to create a vision board for your future growth and the life you want.

I would like you to take a few moments to really think about your intentions. Consider the aspects of your shadow self that you want to envision for yourself in the future.

 Write down your intentions in a clear and concise manner. For example, "I intend to explore and heal my suppressed emotions, fears, and limiting beliefs while manifesting a brighter, more authentic future."

_____

_____

_____

_____

Gather the materials you'll need for your vision board:

- Poster board or a large piece of cardboard.

- Scissors.

- Glue or adhesive.

- Magazines, images, and words that resonate with both your shadow work and your desired future.

- Markers, colored pencils, or other art supplies (optional).

Start flipping through magazines, books, or online resources to find images and words that resonate with both your shadow self and your vision for the future. Look for pictures that represent your suppressed emotions, fears, or the aspects of yourself you want to continue to work on. Additionally, find images and words that symbolize the positive changes and growth you want to achieve.

Now, it's time to assemble your vision board:

- Cut out the images and words that you've selected.

- Arrange them on your poster board in a way that feels visually appealing and meaningful to you. You can create sections or clusters to represent different aspects of your journey.

- Start gluing the images and words onto the poster board. As you do this, reflect on the significance of each item and how it relates to your shadow work and your desired future.

- You can get creative by adding colors, drawings, or personal touches that enhance the board's emotional resonance.

Once your vision board is complete, take some time to sit with it. Close your eyes, take a few deep breaths, and meditate on the images and words you've chosen. Allow yourself to connect with the emotions and intentions you've set for your shadow work and your future growth.

Place your vision board in a prominent and visible location where you'll see it daily. This serves as a powerful reminder of your intentions and can help keep you focused and motivated on your shadow work and your journey toward personal growth and healing.

In this chapter, we covered a great deal of fear, anxiety, hope, and motivation. As we conclude this last chapter, I want to remind you that the journey of shadow work is not always easy, but it is undeniably worth it. You have the tools to do the work, and now you know how to stay on track.

Unveiling The Shadows: A Call To Share Your Journey

In the realm of shadow work, solidarity and understanding are invaluable treasures. When you leave a review, you send an echo of support into the void, letting others know that their struggles and victories are acknowledged and shared. This sense of community is vital in a journey that can often feel isolating.

So, I call upon you, brave navigators of the inner self, to share your journey, to leave a review for this self-guided shadow work workbook and journal for beginners. Let your voice be heard, your journey acknowledged, and your wisdom shared. In doing so, you not only affirm your growth and transformation but also extend a hand to those still navigating their way through the shadows.

YOU CAN HELP OTHERS!

Thank you so much for your support. We all need a helping hand from time to time and your words could be the spark that ignites someone's transformation.

Scan the QR code to leave your review!

Conclusion

As we come to the end of this workbook, I want to remind you of the incredible journey you've embarked upon. Throughout these pages, you've ventured deep into the realm of shadow work, bravely confronting the shadows that have silently haunted you for so long. You've walked through the corridors of your past, where painful memories lurked, faced the storm of challenging emotions, and challenged the limitations of your beliefs with courage and unwavering determination. It's been an incredible journey, and now, it's time to distill the essence of what you've learned.

In this process, you've discovered a profound truth—your shadows are not your adversaries; they are an integral part of you. By acknowledging, embracing, and owning them, you are taking control of your own healing and personal growth. They are not your enemies, but rather, they are the stepping stones toward your wholeness.

Remember Liz, whom we met at the beginning of this workbook? Her story may resonate with the struggles you've encountered on your own path. Liz, much like you, found herself stuck in a relentless cycle of pain and confusion. She, too, harbored doubts and fears about embarking on the journey of shadow work, worrying that it might exacerbate her already heavy burdens. With courage, she took that leap of faith, just as you have. And as she progressed down this path, she started to notice the subtle but profound shifts in her life.

The heavy burden of her past began to lift, layer by layer, revealing the light that was hidden beneath. She realized that she could navigate this transformative journey at her own pace, forging her own support system along the way. Her story is a testament to the power of shadow work to bring about positive change, even in the face of doubt and fear.

Now, it's your turn to celebrate your progress. Take a moment to look back on the breakthroughs you've achieved, no matter how seemingly insignificant they may appear. Every step you've taken, every shadow you've confronted, has propelled you forward on your path to healing and self-discovery.

Share your newfound wisdom and awareness with others who may be on a similar journey. Offer them guidance, support, and encouragement, just as you've received along the way. Remember that personal growth is not a destination but a lifelong journey, and every effort you make to heal is a significant victory in itself.

If you found this workbook helpful on your journey, I invite you to consider leaving a review or sharing your experiences with others. By doing so, you can help ensure that this workbook reaches the hands of those just beginning their own path of shadow work. Your words may be the very encouragement someone else needs to take that courageous step forward in their healing journey.

So, continue to shine your light brightly, moving forward into the life you are so inherently worthy of. Your journey is a testament to your inner strength and resilience. Each new day brings you closer to a brighter, more authentic life. Thank you for allowing me to be a part of your shadow work journey, and may your path be forever illuminated with growth, healing, and love.

Other Books You'll Love By

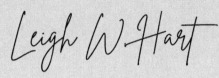

Leigh W. Hart

Don't Get Derailed By Your Attachment Style

Whether you are anxious, avoidant, or fearful in relationships, this book will provide you with proven strategies for effectively dealing with an insecure attachment style.

#1 Best Seller

Reparenting Your Wounded Inner Child

Explore Childhood and Generational Trauma to Break Destructive Patterns, Build Emotional Strength and Achieve Personal Growth with 7 Empowering Steps. Free yourself from the pains of the past and create a life you will love now and in the future.

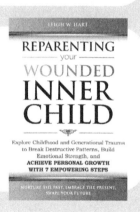

CBT Inner Child Workbook   *Available Fall 2024*

Heal Past Trauma, Restore Emotional Resilience, and Reclaim Your Joy with Cognitive Behavioral Therapy Exercises, Journal Prompts, and Self-love Practices. This workbook is your companion on the journey to nurture and heal your inner child.

Advanced Self-Guided Shadow Work

Transcend basic self-reflection and move towards profound self-awareness with this advanced shadow workbook and journal. Venture into your own depths and find untapped reservoirs of resilience, strength, and insight.

Available June 2024

Amazon.com/Author/LeighWHart

My GIFT to you!

Elevate Your Journey...
with BONUS
Complimentary Support Materials

GIFT #1: Self-Assessment Tests & Bonus Materials

As you begin your shadow work journey, are you unsure where to focus your efforts? Use the self-assessment tests to determine which areas of your life need the most attention.

GIFT #2: Sneak Peek, plus 10 Advanced Shadow Work Exercises

Get a sneak peek inside "Advanced Self-Guided Shadow Work" to continue your journey with an even deeper exploration into your shadow's subconscious. Includes: 10 Advanced Shadow Work exercises!

GIFT #3: The Evolving Growth Workbook

Personal growth is a lifelong journey. Use this workbook now and in the future to revisit insights learned, reevaluate your progress, and continue evolving on your path to personal fulfillment.

Go to:
ShadowWork.LeighWHart.com
to receive your BONUS printable support materials.

References

Ackerman, C. (2019, June 21). What is self-regulation? (+95 skills and strategies). PositivePsychology.com. https://positivepsychology.com/self-regulation/

Akbari, K. (2023, July 18). Shadow work prompts for insecurity. Eye Mind Spirit. https://www.eyemindspirit.com/post/shadow-work-prompts-for-insecurity

Anderson, O. (n.d.). Oli Anderson quotes. Goodreads. https://www.goodreads.com/work/quotes/85809606-shadow-life-freedom-from-an-unreal-world---reclaim-your-hidden-self-pr#:~:text=Shadow%20Life%3A%20Freedom%20from%20an,World%20%2D%20Reclaim%20Your...&text=Your%20Shadow%20is%20all%20of,forgot%20that%20you're%20wearing.

BetterHelp Editorial Team. (2023, October 10). Introspection guide. Betterhelp. https://www.betterhelp.com/advice/psychologists/what-is-introspection-psychology-definition-and-applications/

Britt Jr, W. B. (2019, October 23). Roleplaying as shadow work. Medium. https://medium.com/@wendell.britt/roleplaying-as-shadow-work-34a072b47da9

Brown, B. (2022, December 5). What is the shadow self + shadow work. Modern Manifestation. https://www.themodernmanifestation.com/post/shadow-work

Cisler, J. M., Olatunji, B. O., Feldner, M. T., & Forsyth, J. P. (2009). Emotion regulation and the anxiety disorders: An integrative review. Journal of Psychopathology and Behavioral Assessment, 32(1), 68–82. https://doi.org/10.1007/s10862-009-9161-1

El Gerbi, Y. (2020, September 2). How I met my shadow self, and how you can meet yours. Curious. https://medium.com/curious/how-i-met-my-shadow-self-and-how-you-can-meet-yours-aea21680c7ff

Ford, D. (n.d.). Debbie Ford quotes. Goodreads. https://www.goodreads.com/author/quotes/7851.Debbie_Ford

For those who have actively engaged in shadow work, what did your process look like? I've read enough theory, and I would like to hear fr... (2021). Quora. https://www.quora.com/For-those-who-have-actively-engaged-in-shadow-work-what-did-your-process-look-like-Ive-read-enough-theory-and-I-would-like-to-hear-from-someone-who-successfully-integrated-their-shadow-in-tangible-reality-and-is-no

Fosu, K. (2020, December 14). Shadow work: A simple guide to transcending the darker aspects of the self. Medium. https://medium.com/big-self-society/shadow-work-a-simple-guide-to-transcending-the-darker-aspects-of-the-self-e948ee285723

Fritscher, L. (2023, April 11). The psychology of fear. Verywell Mind. https://www.verywellmind.com/the-psychology-of-fear-2671696

Graham, S. (n.d.). Sasha Graham quotes. Goodreads. https://www.goodreads.com/quotes/10314300-the-shadow-is-needed-now-more-than-ever-we-heal

Griffiths, N. (2021, September 15). 40 powerful affirmations for shadow work. Seeking Serotonin. https://seekingserotonin.com/affirmations-for-shadow-work/#google_vignette

Grinspoon, P. (2022, May 4). How to recognize and tame your cognitive distortions. Harvard Health. https://www.health.harvard.edu/blog/how-to-recognize-and-tame-your-cognitive-distortions-202205042738

Guil, R., Gómez-Molinero, R., Merchán-Clavellino, A., & Gil-Olarte, P. (2021). Lights and shadows of trait emotional intelligence: Its mediating role in the relationship between negative affect and state anxiety in university students. Frontiers in Psychology, 11. https://doi.org/10.3389/fpsyg.2020.615010

How to integrate your shadow – the dark side is unrealized potential. (2020, February 27). Academy of Ideas. https://academyofideas.com/2020/02/how-to-integrate-your-shadow/

Identifying triggers worksheet & example. (2023). Carepatron. https://www.carepatron.com/templates/identifying-triggers-worksheet

Ingram, J. (2022, May 9). Cost remains significant barrier to therapy access, Verywell Mind survey finds. Verywell Mind. https://www.verywellmind.com/cost-of-therapy-survey-5271327

Keng, S. L., Smoski, M. J., & Robins, C. J. (2011). Effects of mindfulness on psychological health: A review of empirical studies. Clinical Psychology Review, 31(6), 1041–1056. https://doi.org/10.1016/j.cpr.2011.04.006

LaVine, R. (2023, March 28). 100+ deep shadow work prompts to accept yourself and move forward. Science of People. https://www.scienceofpeople.com/shadow-work-prompts/

Mani, M. (2017, September 28). 12 short stories on self realization and finding your true self. OutofStress. https://www.outofstress.com/self-realization-short-stories/

Mayer, B. A. (2023, October 10). Shadow work: Can TikTok's self-care trend improve your mental health? Healthline. https://www.healthline.com/health-news/how-the-shadow-work-tiktok-trend-can-help-your-mental-health

Margery, M. (2023, February 2). Unless you learn to face your own shadow. The Minds Journal. https://themindsjournal.com/quotes/unless-learn-face-shadow/

Othon, J. (2017, October 20). Carl Jung and the shadow: The ultimate guide to the human dark side. HighExistence. https://www.highexistence.com/carl-jung-shadow-guide-unconscious/

Pedersen, T. (2022, May 6). 7 tips for improving your self-awareness. Psych Central. https://psychcentral.com/health/how-to-be-more-self-aware-and-why-its-important

Projection. (2022, January 5). Psychology Today. https://www.psychologytoday.com/ca/basics/projection

Regan, S. (2021, November 11). How to embrace & integrate your shadow self for major healing. Mindbodygreen. https://www.mindbodygreen.com/articles/shadow-self

"Safe place" relaxation exercise. (2019, October 30). Spring Psychology. https://www.springpsychology.co.uk/post/safe-place-relaxation-exercise

St. Catherine of Siena. (n.d.). St. Catherine of Siena quotes. AZ Quotes. https://www.azquotes.com/quote/818366

Sansone, R. A., Leung, J. S., & Wiederman, M. W. (2012). Five forms of childhood trauma. The Primary Care Companion for CNS Disorders, 14. https://doi.org/10.4088/pcc.12m01353

7 ways to spot your shadow self - inner shadow work. (2021, July 17). Inner Shadow Work. https://innershadowwork.com/7-ways-to-spot-your-shadow-self-2/

Shadow integration 101. (2019, April 3). The Lovett Center. https://thelovettcenter.com/shadow-integration-101/

Stutz, P. (2022, November 7). How to bond with your shadow. THE TOOLS. https://www.thetoolsbook.com/blog/how-to-bond-with-your-shadow

Sweeney, A., Filson, B., Kennedy, A., Collinson, L., & Gillard, S. (2018). A paradigm shift: relationships in trauma-informed mental health services. BJPsych Advances, 24(5), 319–333. https://doi.org/10.1192/bja.2018.29

Tagore, R. (n.d.). Rabindranath Tagore quotes. Goodreads. https://www.goodreads.com/work/quotes/2676430-stray-birds

Taibbi, R. (2023, August 4). How to be your own therapist. Psychology Today. https://www.psychologytoday.com/za/blog/fixing-families/202308/how-to-be-your-own-therapist

Tartakovsky, M. (2014, September 22). Embracing your dark side. Psych Central. https://psychcentral.com/blog/owning-our-dark-sides#benefits

Thakur, P. (2019, June 19). Top 10 inspirational success stories. YourStory.com. https://yourstory.com/mystory/top-10-inspirational-success-stories

Tracking progress in therapy matters (and how to do it). (2023, October 17). Www.sondermind.com. https://www.sondermind.com/resources/why-tracking-your-therapy-progress-matters-and-how-to-do-it

Veazey, K. (2022, May 3). Emotional self-regulation: Importance, problems, and strategies. MedicalNewsToday. https://www.medicalnewstoday.com/articles/emotional-self-regulation

Villines, Z. (2022, August 30). What is shadow work? Benefits and exercises. MedicalNewsToday. https://www.medicalnewstoday.com/articles/what-is-shadow-work#:~:text=Shadow%20work%20is%20a%20type

Images

Images on the following pages were created with the assistance of DALL-E-2: 12, 19, 22, 25, 27, 34, 45, 55, 56, 71, 82, 94, 104, 113, 124, 134, and 156.

Images on the following pages were created with the assistance of Midjourney: 24, 35, 37, 40, 50, 69, 97, 152, 185, 209, and 219.

Printed in Great Britain
by Amazon

43552853R00132